Do and Discover Science

by Marilee Woodfield

illustrated by Janet Armbrust

Publisher
Key Education Publishing Company, LLC
Minneapolis, Minnesota

CONGRATULATIONS ON YOUR PURCHASE OF A KEY EDUCATION PRODUCT!

The editors at Key Education are former teachers who bring experience, enthusiasm, and quality to each and every product. Thousands of teachers have looked to the staff at Key Education for new and innovative resources to make their work more enjoyable and rewarding. We are committed to developing educational materials that will assist teachers in building a strong and developmentally appropriate curriculum for young children.

PLAN FOR GREAT TEACHING EXPERIENCES WHEN YOU USE EDUCATIONAL MATERIALS FROM KEY EDUCATION PUBLISHING COMPANY, LLC

Credits

Author: Marilee Woodfield
Publisher: Sherrill B. Flora
Editors: Debra Pressnall and Kelly Huxmann
Inside Illustrations: Janet Armbrust
Page Design and Layout: Debra Pressnall
Cover Design: Annette Hollister-Papp
Photo Credits: Photo www.comstock.com, © Brand X Pictures, © ShutterStock, and © Photodisc

Key Education welcomes manuscripts and product ideas from teachers. For a copy of our submission guidelines, please send a self-addressed stamped envelope to: Key Education Publishing Company, LLC Acquisitions Department 9601 Newton Avenue South Minneapolis, Minnesota 55431

About the Author

Marilee Woodfield graduated with a bachelor of science in human development from Brigham Young University. In addition to teaching and directing preschools for 20 years, she has written more than 15 resource books for early childhood educators. Marilee also spends her time teaching after-school science classes for elementary students, driving the family taxi service, and engaging in various home-improvement projects. She currently resides in Texas with her husband and four children.

Copyright Notice

Standard Book Number: 1-933052-29-5
Do and Discover Science
Copyright © 2007 by Key Education Publishing Company, LLC
Minneapolis, Minnesota 55431

TABLE OF CONTENTS

INTRODUCTION

Children are naturally inquisitive and learn best through hands-on experiences. If the study of science is simply a process of curiosity, then it makes sense that children would be attracted to science concepts and activities. Each learning theme in this book highlights how science can be part of young children's everyday experiences. The lessons present important science concepts in a simple format that is easy for children to understand, yet challenges them to use higher-level thought processes. Even though children may not think about specific science skills while exploring, observing, classifying, and communicating about how things act in certain situations, they are still using those skills to understand the world around them.

Here are some ways to get the most out of this resource book while helping young learners acquire necessary science skills:

- **Encourage children to ask questions.** You can use the questions that appear at the beginning of activity suggestions to engage your budding scientists. And when the activity is finished, find out what other related questions the children may have that can be tested with simple experiments.

- **Remember that science is a method for acquiring knowledge.** While this book includes many suggestions for "free exploration" along with demonstration ideas and structured group activities, do not hesitate to let the children tackle any project you feel they can complete safely. (Resign yourself to allowing the children to make a mess—science can be messy. However, messes can be managed easily by providing paper towels and newspaper for spills when working with water, and by directing children to return equipment to storage tubs when finished.) Allowing children the freedom to explore will strengthen understanding of science concepts.

- **Talk with the children as they work.** Find out what they already know about the topic as well as any misconceptions they may have. As the children investigate, encourage them to explain their observations and think of new questions they would like to answer. By taking an active role and asking guiding questions, you will help children acquire science process skills and learn how to be better communicators. Use related vocabulary words for each theme often. It may seem strange for children to understand such "big" words, but before you know it, they will be using those words independently.

- **Record what is being observed.** Second only to actual hands-on exploration, one of the key parts of science investigation is recording information. My Science Plan on page 7 can be used as a guide when recording what the children are learning. Use it as a tool to teach language and writing, and, of course, make it interactive and visual. Record the main points on chart paper and then fill in the information when everyone gathers to discuss their observations. Attach pertinent pieces of equipment, pictures drawn by the children, and samples of data (items in zippered plastic bags) whenever possible. You may even consider enlarging the outline to poster size for each theme and creating a "big book" as a reminder of what science topics the children have studied.

- **Extend the lessons.** Use letters to families to encourage additional science investigations at home. Several themes in this book include letters that you can photocopy and send home to encourage parents to become involved in what is happening in your classroom.

- **Read aloud science books and other related literature to the children whenever possible.** This will stimulate language acquisition and reinforce what the children have observed during "science play." A few literature selections have been provided for each theme. Check with your school librarian for other recommendations.

Above all, enjoy the activities and experiments in this book. And do not forget to be a little curious yourself—you just never know what you will discover. After all, that is what "doing science" is all about: meaningful learning that is a lot of fun, too!

SCIENCE TOOLS

There are several tools that are very useful during science explorations. Ruler, eyedropper, magnifying glass, and a balance are all common science tools that children can learn how to use. Organize your science center so that each of these tools is available for individual exploration during center time. If appropriate, demonstrate how to use each tool and designate a specific place or storage tub for it. Here are some easy activities to engage busy little hands in manipulating these science tools:

Magnifying Glass

Provide a large magnifying glass and a variety of objects, such as bug specimens, leaves, rocks, feathers, photographs, or theme-related objects in the science center. Have the children use the magnifying glass to examine the objects and then talk about what they see. Everything looks very different when enlarged!

Balance

Locate a balance that has two small buckets for holding objects. Then assemble a set of small plastic math counters (plastic cubes, identical animal shapes, etc.) that can be used for comparison. Encourage the children to select objects from the classroom and find out how much they weigh by putting an object in one balance bucket and filling the other bucket with identical math counters.

Ruler

Collect several items of various lengths for the children to measure. Have them use a ruler or, if appropriate, nonstandard units of measurement such as wooden or plastic blocks.

Eyedropper

Fill three jars with water and use food coloring to color them red, yellow, and blue. Place an eyedropper, paper towels, and a polystyrene egg carton near the jars of colored water in a storage tray. Have the child use the eyedropper to take water from one jar and place several drops in one of the egg-carton cavities. Ask the child to predict what will happen if a certain color is added to the water drops. Then guide the child to test that prediction. Encourage the children to see how many different colors they can create by mixing the colors. Use the paper towels to absorb excess water when new colors are mixed. As an added bonus, this activity will help children strengthen their fine motor skills.

ACTIVE SCIENCE

When making science explorations, children need to learn and apply these four important steps:

STEP 1: QUESTION

What do you want to know? It is important for children to clarify what they want to learn in the form of a question. This is the first step, and a very important one, in thinking like a scientist. Questions such as "What will happen when I drop a ball?" "Why is it dark at night?" or "What happens to seeds that grow?" can be answered with simple tests. To demonstrate, try this experiment:

Pose the question, "What happens when you poke a water-filled balloon with a pin?"

STEP 2: PREDICT

This step of the process is also called making a "hypothesis." When you predict an outcome, you are simply tapping into what you already know in order to make an inference about something you are not sure about. For example, when conducting the balloon experiment, the children are probably very aware that pins can pop balloons. (You may want to demonstrate this outcome on one balloon to see if that is right.) Therefore, they could easily predict the results to this experiment. However, there are always variables that can affect the outcome.

The children predict what will happen if a water-filled balloon is poked with a pin.

STEP 3: TEST

After you have considered what you want to learn and have made a prediction (or guess, if a preschooler) about the outcome, the next step is to test or try out your ideas. Even when you are pretty sure about the results, it is important to test things, just like a good scientist does. Comparing, contrasting, sorting, observing, and classifying are also part of this process.

Poke a water-filled balloon with a pin.

STEP 4: REFLECT

New or confirmed information is gained in this step of the process. By conducting the test, you found out that your prediction was either accurate or incorrect, and you may have to repeat steps 1, 2, and 3 because new questions emerged after conducting the experiment.

A water-filled balloon leaks water when poked with a pin.

By completing My Science Plan on page 7 for an activity, children can become familiar with the process of asking a question, predicting an outcome, testing their ideas, and reflecting on what they have learned.

Science Safety

Here are some safety tips to follow when doing science activities:

- Always follow your teacher's directions.

- Never smell or taste a project *unless your teacher says it is okay.*

- Always clean up when you are finished.

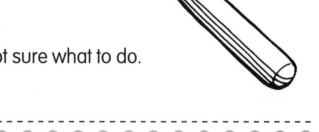

- Ask a grown-up for help if you are not sure what to do.

✂ —

● ●

Name _____ Date _____

 My Science Plan

What if . . .?	I am predicting that . . .
I will test my ideas by . . .	I discovered . . .

AMAZING AIR

MATERIALS

- 3 clear plastic drinking cups
- drinking straw, paint, and finger-paint paper
- duct tape
- food coloring
- garbage bags
- jumbo-sized craft sticks
- new pencils
- paper towels
- pattern (page 11)
- plastic streamers, dowels, and duct tape
- pushpins
- scissors
- small paper plates
- transparent bucket
- various lightweight objects
- water
- watercolor markers or crayons

BOOKS TO SHARE

- *Air Is All Around You* by Franklyn M. Branley (HarperTrophy, 1986)
- *How Does the Wind Walk?* by Nancy White Carlstrom (MacMillan, 1993)
- *I Face the Wind* by Vickie Cobb (HarperCollins, 2003)

Background Information

Surrounding the Earth is a blanket of air that is made up of a mixture of gases. Even though we cannot see the air that envelops us, it takes up space, exerts pressure, and at times moves things.

During the following explorations, the children will discover how containers that appear empty are actually filled with air, which escapes in bubbles when held underwater. The children will also feel the force of air when pressing on inflated balloons or plastic bags, and discover how moving air can actually do work by watching lightweight objects "sail" across a smooth surface or observe how things in nature move when it is windy.

Objectives

- Test "empty" containers to find out if air is present
- Recognize that air takes up space
- Demonstrate how air can move some objects

Getting Ready

- Tape paper plates to jumbo-sized craft sticks to make fans for the children to decorate.
- Make a copy of the pinwheel pattern for each child.
- Using a piece of duct tape, attach a plastic streamer to one end of each dowel for the "Air Walk."
- Fill a bucket with water. Add a few drops of food coloring to the water.
- Inflate a large, black plastic garbage bag with air.

EXPLORATIONS

Air on the Move — *How can air be watched?*

Air is everywhere. You cannot see it, but it is there! We do not feel it because it pushes against our bodies equally in all directions. Have the children wave their hands in the air. Explain to the children that they are feeling air moving around their hands because their hands are pushing against the air. Discuss with them how it is possible to feel the air when it is windy.

Science Center: Free Exploration—Provide small paper-plate fans and a variety of lightweight objects, such as cotton balls and small toy cars. How would you wave the paper-plate fan to make the [name of small object] move across the table/floor?

EXPLORATIONS (CONTINUED) ● ● ● ● ● ● ● ● ●

Wind Detectors

How can you tell which way the air is moving?

A simple way to detect air is by watching how a pinwheel moves. If manufactured pinwheels are not available for the children to use, have them make their own. Provide a copy of the pattern on page II for each child. Have the children color their pinwheels as desired. To assemble each pinwheel, first cut along the dashed lines around the square and toward the center of the shape. Then take each corner marked with a small dot and bring it toward the center of the pinwheel, overlapping each one until all specified corners are lightly folded over. (See diagrams on page II as needed.) Force a pushpin through all the layers of the paper and then press it into the eraser of a new pencil. Now the children are ready to use their pinwheels as "Air Detectors."

Science Center: Free Exploration—On a day when there is a gentle breeze, move your "science center" outdoors and have the children take an "Air Walk." First, arrange the dowels with plastic streamers in a straight line across a small area of the playground by inserting one end of each dowel into the ground. After everyone has had an opportunity to watch how the streamers move in the wind, ask the children to suggest where they would like to move the dowels for further observations. Continue the exploration by taking the children on an "Air Walk" around the playground to observe how other things are moved by the wind. Be sure to bring along the pinwheel Air Detectors, too!

Magic Cups

Does air take up space?

Because air is everywhere, it takes up space. Have the children gather around you to look at three "empty" drinking cups. First, ask the children to describe what they see when looking at the cups. Record their observations on chart paper. Take a piece of paper towel and stuff it into the bottom of one clear cup. Let all the children put their hands in the cup to feel the paper towel. Record some of their comments. Ask the children to predict what will happen to the paper towel if you pour water into the cup and then test their ideas. Be sure to record these observations, too. Allow the children to feel the paper towel now that it is wet.

Demonstrate what happens when the second plastic drinking cup is inverted and submerged in the water. To do this, first, stuff a paper towel into the bottom of the second cup. Explain that you are going to put the cup in the water upside down and ask the children to predict whether the paper towel will become wet or stay dry. Record their ideas. Place the container of water where all the children can see it. Tip the cup upside down and push it directly into the water. Lift the cup straight back out and remove the paper towel. Let the children feel the towel and note how the towel is dry. Since there was no place for the air to go, the air stayed in the cup and kept the towel dry. Repeat the procedure with the third cup by inserting it upside down into the water and then  tilting it slightly. Have the children observe the bubbles of air leaving the cup as it fills with water.

Science Table: Free Exploration—Allow the children to try this experiment with a dishpan or bucket of water, or have them work at the water table. Alternatively, provide a variety of small plastic containers, such as clean, plastic soda bottles, that the children can submerge in the water to watch how air bubbles float up to the surface. You may also have the children submerge cups filled with small rocks to watch bubbles escaping.

CROSS-CURRICULAR FUN

Air Bag Volley

Show the children the large garbage bag that has been inflated with air. Tell them that you have something very special inside the bag. After the children take turns guessing what might be in the bag, reveal the contents by "pouring" it over their heads. Discuss how air was taking up space inside the bag.

Play a game of air bag volley with your class. Pull the garbage bag through the air to fill it and knot the end of the bag to make a "ball" of air. Alternatively, supply several air bags for the children to use. Draw a line across the center of the classroom with masking tape. Divide the class in half and have one group stand on one side of the line, while the other group faces them on the opposite side. Have the children try to hit the air bags over the line. Increase the difficulty by creating a circle out of masking tape on both sides of the line. Record a tally mark each time a team hits the bag into the opposing team's circle. After a predetermined amount of time, count the tally marks for each team. Switch sides and try again.

Blowing Paint Art

Create unusual splatter-paint pictures by blowing through drinking straws to move drops of tempera paint in different directions. First, scatter large drops of tempera paint on finger-paint paper. Then have a blast moving the paint to make different shapes and some new paint colors, too!

Name _____   Date _____

Take-Home Activity

Watching Air Bubble Up!

Dear Families,

During science time today, we discovered how air fills up spaces between things and inside containers. Please help your child do more exploring by submerging "empty" plastic containers in water to watch for bubbles escaping. This investigation can be done easily in the kitchen sink, a bathtub, dishpan, or even small wading pool. If you have any empty plastic water bottles, perhaps your child could use them as science tools for this activity. Plastic cups work well, too.

When finished, have your child write or draw a picture about what was discovered on the back of this paper before returning it to school.

Thank you for your assistance,

Pinwheel Pattern

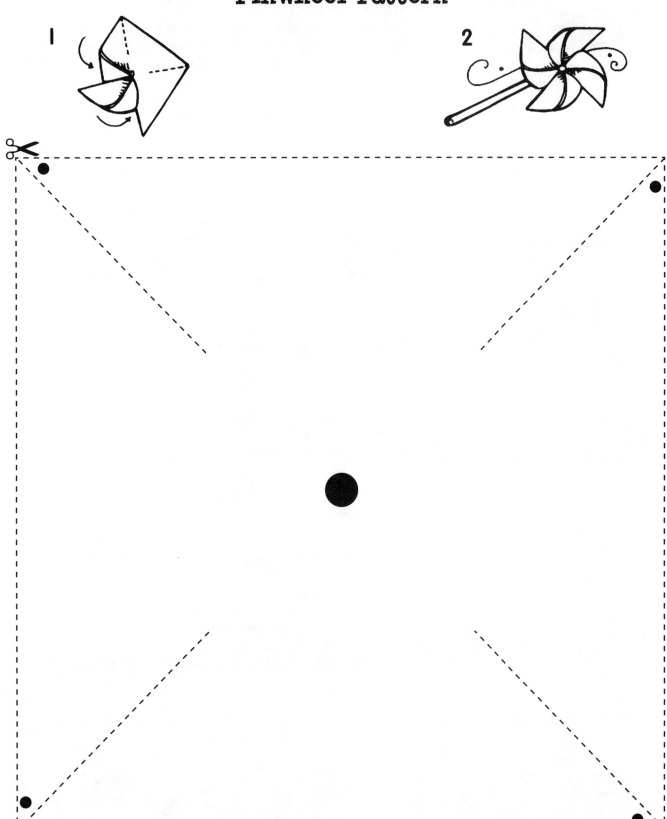

WATER WONDER

Background Information

Water is a marvelous clear liquid that has several distinguishing properties. During the following explorations, children will discover that water molecules are not only attracted to each other (*cohesion*), but they are also attracted to other materials (*adhesion*). Because of its cohesive property, water sticks to other water molecules to form water droplets that can run off smooth surfaces. Have you ever wondered how it is possible to pile up water drops on an object such as a penny? The stickiness between the molecules that creates a "skin" around the water drop makes it possible. This watery skin known as *surface tension* can also be observed when insects "skate" across pond water. As children squirt water on objects to find out which ones absorb water, they are actually investigating the adhesive property of water. This attraction is slightly stronger than the "stickiness" between water molecules making it possible for water to cling to tiny fibers and move up a paper towel strip.

MATERIALS

- 2 large transparent containers
- 3 ft. (1 m) length of clear aquarium tubing
- absorbent paper towels
- black marker
- dishpan
- eyedroppers
- food coloring
- household sponges
- magnifying glass
- newspaper
- objects made from a variety of materials: cloth, paper, wood, metal, ceramic, plastic
- scissors
- simple balance
- small cups
- toothpicks
- turkey baster
- water
- waxed paper

Objectives

- Test different materials to find out which ones will absorb water
- Observe how water is attracted to plastic tubing
- Observe how water drops are attracted to other water drops
- Observe how water will travel up a paper towel
- Demonstrate how small water drops have a rounded shape

Getting Ready

- Cut up large sponges into identical pieces.
- Fill a large container with water. Use food coloring to color the water.
- Fill a small cup with water for each child.
- Tear a sheet of waxed paper for each child.
- Cover the science table with a thick layer of newspaper to help absorb spills.
- Cut paper towels into narrow strips about 2 in. (5 cm) wide.

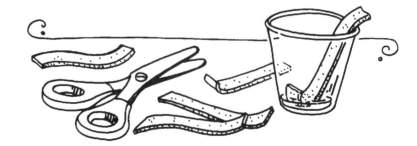

BOOKS TO SHARE

- *Water* by Frank Asch (Voyager Books, 2000)
- *Water's Way* by Lisa Westberg Peters (Arcade Publishing, 1991)

EXPLORATIONS • • • • • •

Making Things Wet

What happens when different things get wet?

Everyone knows that water makes things wet, but what happens if you spray water on toys? Do they change? Does paper change when it gets wet? Gather an assortment of objects made from different kinds of materials, such as an old coloring book, metal and plastic toys, a wood block, newspaper, a plastic dish, a sponge, and a plastic plate. Place the collection of objects along with a large, clear container on the science table. Fill a small bucket with water.

Ask a child to choose one object from the table. Then have the other children describe its properties (e.g., made of metal and plastic) and predict how the object might change when it is wet. Place the object in the clear container and have the children take turns using the turkey baster to squirt water onto it. Repeat the investigation with other objects. Talk about what happened to each object. Also discuss the group of objects collectively. Which kinds of objects absorb or soak up water, and which ones repel water? (Objects like towels, sponges, and newspaper absorb water and become heavier. They also look and feel wet. Some of the water can be squeezed out of these materials. Objects like metal and plastic toys repel the water drops.)

Science Table: Free Exploration—Follow up the lesson by having the children select new objects to test: some that will absorb water and some that will repel it. Direct the children to make predictions and then test their ideas by squirting water onto the objects with a turkey baster. Alternatively, provide dry paper towels, identical pieces of sponges, a bucket balance, dishpan, and container of water on the science table. *Question to investigate:* Are wet sponges heavier than dry sponges? Have the children test their ideas.

Dragging Water Drops

Why do water drops quickly join other water drops?

Observing the shape of water drops and how they move on waxed paper is a simple investigation for children. To begin the exploration, provide colored water, eyedroppers, and pieces of waxed paper. Encourage the children to observe large and small drops of water on the waxed paper. Be sure to include magnifying glasses for a closer view. *Question to investigate:* Will tiny water drops have the same shape as very large drops? Allow the children to test their ideas. When they are finished looking at the drops of water, have them let the water run into a larger container to observe how droplets move across waxed paper.

Now place two drops on the waxed paper close together. Using the toothpick, drag the second drop over to the first. Water likes to stick together. Continue adding and dragging drops. Then place a paper towel on the spot and watch how the colored water is absorbed by the fibers of the paper towel.

Soak It Up!

What happens if one edge of a paper towel is placed in water?

Science Center: Free Exploration—Hang long, narrow paper-towel strips over the edge of a container containing a small amount of water. The bottom of each paper strip should just barely touch the surface of the water. In a few minutes the children will notice the paper towels becoming wet as the water climbs up the strips. Encourage the children to repeat the test several times to find out if the results are the same.

EXPLORATIONS (CONTINUED)

Follow the Leader   *Does water like to play "Follow the Leader"?*

Because water molecules like to stick together, they are great at following each other around. Have the children practice playing "Follow the Leader" by asking one child to lead the rest of the children around the room, weaving in and around furniture.

Continue the lesson by having the children investigate what happens when water plays "Follow the Leader." Place the large transparent container filled with colored water where all the children can see it. Show the children the empty plastic aquarium tubing. Stick one end of the tubing in the large water container, and place the other end in a smaller empty container. Observe what happens. (Nothing.) The tubing is like a big straw, but since there is no water in the tubing, none of the water in the container wants to follow it through the tube into the second container.

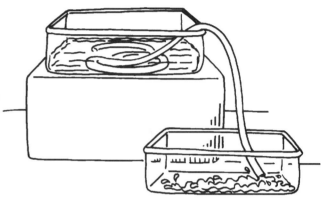

Now immerse the tubing in the container of colored water until the entire tube is filled with water. Place a thumb over one end of the tubing to keep the water inside the tube, and hold the other end of the tube underwater. Take the first end and place it in the smaller empty container at a lower level. Release the water by removing your thumb. The water should begin to siphon into the second container. The water is following other water molecules into the second container through the tube.

CROSS-CURRICULAR FUN

Water Drop Art

• Fill several jars or small plastic cups with water. Use food coloring to make each container a different color.
• Using eyedroppers, drop water onto the waxed paper as desired.
• Carefully lay a paper towel over the colored water to create a beautifully colored piece of art.
• If interested, use a black watercolor marker to add additional details after the paper has dried.

SOLIDS AND LIQUIDS

MATERIALS

- 2 differently shaped clear plastic containers
- apple and book, ball, or wood block
- colored water
- corn syrup
- duct tape
- eyedroppers
- household sponges
- ingredients to make cupcakes
- magnifying glass
- metallic confetti
- milk and vinegar
- paper cups
- soybeans or dried beans
- various objects to sort by properties (see Getting Ready)
- variety of containers
- vegetable oil
- water table and supplies for exploration
- waxed paper
- zippered plastic bags

BOOK TO SHARE

- *What Is the World Made Of? All About Solids, Liquids, and Gases* by Kathleen Weidner Zoehfeld (HarperTrophy, 1998)

Background Information

The world of solids and liquids is quite fascinating for children. Their life experiences probably include scooping sand and rocks into buckets, filling containers with water, taking a shower, eating snacks, playing with cars and trucks, building towers with blocks, painting pictures with watercolors, washing their hands, and floating toy boats in water. Solids and liquids are part of children's everyday experiences, so it is necessary for them to deepen their understanding about matter.

Even though solids and liquids both take up space and have mass, they also have other unique properties. During the study of this theme, children will no doubt have lots of observations they can share because of their experiences with matter. Before beginning an investigation, find out more about the children's prior knowledge by discussing and recording their ideas on chart paper. Solids are easy for children to identify. Perhaps they have not thought about how solids always keep their shapes even when pushed, pulled, or dumped into containers. On the other hand, liquids do not have recognizable shapes. They take the shapes of the containers holding them, as children will discover when completing the activity "Going with the Flow." Liquids also have a readiness to flow. Some liquids, such as water, apple juice, vinegar, and oil, flow easily, while other liquids, like honey or corn syrup, have a resistance to flow.

Objectives

- Observe that solids have definite shapes and cannot be poured
- Identify and describe solids by the materials used to make them
- Observe how liquids take the shapes of their containers and flow downward
- Identify and describe the properties of liquids

Getting Ready

- Gather a variety of simple solids in two or three different colors for the children to sort. Suggestions include tennis balls, golf balls, marbles, plastic and wooden beads (spheres and cubes), plastic and wooden blocks, paper clips or other metallic objects, magnetic balls, and sponges cut up into small cubes. This way, even though the objects are different, a young child could sort the solids in various ways: by color, size, or shape. Make identical sorting bags with an assortment of objects, one bag for each group of children.
- Fill small zippered plastic bags one-third full of red-colored water. Make a second set of zippered bags partially filled with red colored corn syrup. Fill a third set of zippered bags with vegetable oil. Seal the openings of the bags securely with duct tape.
- After completing the solid explorations, fill the water table with water and gather water exploration tools and equipment.
- Collect three or four small, clear water bottles. Fill each one with a different liquid, such as vegetable oil, corn syrup, vinegar, and water. Before placing the caps on the bottles, add the same number of colorful metallic confetti pieces to each liquid. Then seal the bottles and tape the caps on securely with duct tape.

EXPLORATIONS • • • • • • • • • • •

It's a Solid!   *What is a solid?*

A solid object is any object that has a definite shape. An apple stays in the shape of an apple and a ball stays in the shape of a ball when held. Place one of the objects, for example, an apple, in a clear plastic container. Note how the apple still has the shape of an apple. Tip the apple onto the table. (It still looks like an apple.) Gently push the apple across the table, or poke at it with your hands. (A solid always stays the same shape, even when we touch, move, or push it.) Continue the lesson with a book, ball, or wood block.

Pass out the sorting bags for the children to explore. Talk about the objects in the bags. Describe them by their properties, such as shape, color, hardness, and material (what they are made of).

Have the children name other things that are solids. List the items on a sheet of poster board. If appropriate, separate the list by the kinds of materials, such as metal, wood, and plastic.

Science Table: Free Exploration—In a large plastic tub, provide various kinds of balls (tennis balls, golf balls, and marbles) in different colors along with a magnifying glass. Encourage the children to examine the balls and think of words to describe them (e.g., The tennis ball is fuzzy, and the marble is smooth and hard). In a second tub, provide plastic and wooden beads and two smaller containers. Invite the children to sort the items into two groups by shape, color, or material and then draw pictures and "write" about what they did.

EXPLORATIONS (CONTINUED)

Solid Explorers
Can I change the shape of a solid?

Have each child find an object in the classroom that is a solid. Encourage the children to manipulate the solid objects by turning them around and over, and pushing, pulling, or poking them. Talk about each object and what makes it a solid. To help children remember what a solid is, use the following questions: Does it have a shape? (Yes.) Does it change when we move or push it? (No.) Drop the objects into a zippered plastic bag and note how they did not change.

Science Table: Free Exploration—Will the shape of a solid such as dried beans or popcorn change if it is poured into a container? Can you completely fill a container with lots of beans? Direct the children to investigate these questions. To get started, provide a large quantity of soybeans or dried beans in a dishpan so the children can explore by filling and emptying various clear containers. Alternatively, allow the children to work at an empty water table and find out if the solids can completely fill up clear containers, cups, and bowls.

Shape Mimics
What is a liquid like?

A liquid is a substance that can be poured and that takes the shape of the container in which it is held. To demonstrate, pour water into a clear container. Show how the liquid assumes the shape of the container. Then pour the same liquid into a second, different-shaped container. (It assumes the shape of that container.) Pour a small amount of water onto the table and have the children observe what happens. (It will begin to spread over the table, taking the flat shape of the table.) Ask the children to name other things that are liquids.

Give each pair of children a zippered plastic bag filled with a little water. Direct the children to place their bags on the floor and explain what happens to the water in the bags. Have the children carefully poke or tip their bags into different positions and shapes. Ask the children, "What happens to the water now?" (Because it is a liquid, it moves and makes new shapes.) Discuss how water that is poured into a bag takes the shape of the bag, and when poured back into a cup, it assumes the shape of the cup again.

Repeat the exploration with the bags containing corn syrup and vegetable oil. Also, pour small drops of corn syrup and oil onto the table for the children to observe. Because the corn syrup resists flowing, it will move very slowly in the bag.

Science Table: Free Exploration—Provide the children with small water bottles filled with various liquids and some colorful metallic confetti pieces. Encourage the children to shake the bottles and watch how the confetti pieces move around in the liquids.

EXPLORATIONS (CONTINUED)

Going with the Flow

Can the shape of a liquid be changed?

Provide a water table along with several measuring cups, clear containers of all sizes and shapes, funnels, slotted spoons, and colanders, and let the children investigate water. At another time, pour a different liquid such as milk into a small dishpan. Encourage the children to pour the liquid from one small container into another one to observe what happens. *Note: Even though homogenized milk is actually an emulsion (colloid), it is a good lesson for young children to observe and identify the liquid properties of milk.*

Alternatively, supply vinegar in a small container along with an empty container that is placed inside a dishpan. Direct the children to pour the vinegar from one container to another. Caution them that vinegar will have a strong odor. Be sure the children wear safety glasses, just like scientists, when they investigate this liquid, and wash their hands carefully afterwards. Talk about how the milk or vinegar poured, dripped, and splashed just like water.

Floating Blobs

Can a liquid float on top of another liquid?

Investigate what happens when vegetable oil is added to a small water bottle filled three-fourths full with blue-colored water. Ask the children, "If vegetable oil is added to water, will the liquids mix together?" Have them predict what will happen before testing their ideas. Using a funnel, pour the oil into the bottle. Leave a small air space so the liquids will move in the bottle when shaken. Place the cap on the bottle and seal it securely with duct tape. Let the children shake the bottle and then watch what happens to the oil.
If the bottle is gently rocked back and forth, the movement of the water and oil may resemble ocean waves.

CROSS-CURRICULAR FUN

Cupcake Science

As a class, make cupcakes for a delicious treat. While preparing the cupcake batter, talk about whether the ingredients are liquids or solids. As you mix the batter in the bowl, explain that you are not only mixing the ingredients together, but also mixing air (a gas) into the batter, which they cannot see. As you pour the batter into the cupcake molds, have the children tell you whether the batter is a solid, liquid, or gas. (It is a liquid because you can pour it and it takes the shape of the cupcake molds.) Bake the cupcake batter as directed in the recipe. When finished baking, the cupcakes have a shape that does not change (solid). Now to find the gas: Break the cupcakes in half. Have the children look closely at the cupcakes. They will see many little holes or pockets inside. Explain how those holes were created by a gas that was trapped inside the batter as the cupcakes were baking. Enjoy your phase-change cupcakes for a snack.

GASES AND BUBBLES

MATERIALS

- baking pan
- balloon
- bubble solution
- clear soda
- clothespin
- drinking straws
- electric mixer and bowl
- food coloring
- ingredients for making colloid-mallows
- paper
- paper towels
- ruler
- small clear cups
- spoon
- sugar
- whipped topping in a pressurized can
- whipping cream
- zippered plastic bags

BOOKS TO SHARE

- *Pop! A Book About Bubbles* by Kimberly Brubaker Bradley (HarperCollins, 2001), includes recipes for bubble solutions
- *What Is the World Made Of? All About Solids, Liquids, and Gases* by Kathleen Weidner Zoehfeld (HarperTrophy, 1998)

Background Information

Floating bubbles, bubble baths, bubbles in sodas, dish-detergent bubbles—bubbles are fun and fascinating! A soap bubble is formed when air is trapped within a wall of soap film. No matter if the wand is circular or oddly shaped, the bubbles will always be shaped like balls due to the amount of surface tension and attraction between molecules in the bubble solution.

If you are interested in making large bubbles, use your favorite recipe or locate one on the Internet. Choose a recipe that contains a liquid dish detergent such as Dawn® or Joy® and glycerin, which can be purchased at a drugstore. The glycerin in the solution slows down the action of water evaporating so the bubbles last longer. When you are ready to make bubbles, select a time when the humidity is not low. This could be during the cool morning hours or after a rain shower. As you blow into the solution and then watch the soap bubbles travel up into the sky, keep in mind that the air inside the bubble is probably warmer than the surrounding body of air. This trapped air is less dense, causing the bubble to float upwards.

Bubbles also appear in carbonated beverages after the liquid is poured into a drinking glass, or when a soda can or bottle is opened. Those bubbles are filled with a clear, odorless gas called *carbon dioxide*. This fizzing action is fun to watch as bubbles float to the surface of the liquid.

Objectives

- Observe how gases take up space and have mass
- Make bubbles by blowing into bubble solution
- Explain how bubbles are formed

Getting Ready

- Open a bottle of bubble solution and pour it into another cup so that the children cannot recognize the solution by the container.
- Alternatively, make your own bubble solution by following your favorite recipe or one offered on the Internet.

EXPLORATIONS • • • • • • • • • • •

Gases

What is a gas?

A gas is a substance that is invisible. You cannot observe it until you fill something with it. Show the children the balloon. It is empty. Now fill the balloon with air and pinch it closed with a clothespin. Let the children squeeze the balloon to feel the air inside. Discuss how the balloon expands because the air (gas) is taking up space and pushing against the walls of the balloon. Even though we cannot see the air inside the balloon, we can feel its force against the balloon when we squeeze it. Remove the clothespin and release the air slowly so the children can feel it coming out of the balloon.

Have the children hold their hands up in front of their faces and blow on them. Ask the children, "What do you feel?" (Even though we cannot see the air, we know it is there because we can feel it on our hands.) Give each child a zippered plastic bag. Direct the children to seal the openings halfway and then blow into the unsealed portion of the bags. When the bags are inflated, direct the children to seal them. Now the children can explore how the gas reacts inside the bags.

Gas Explorers

What does a gas look like?

We know that gases are invisible. However, when we mix them with other things, like juice, we can sometimes see bubbles of gas. Pour the carbonated soda into a clear cup. Show the children the bubbles and talk about how the bubbles are filled with a special gas (*carbon dioxide*) that has been added to the soda. If the bubbles float to the top of the liquid, they will pop out into the air. Gases can carry scents with them. Tell the children to wave their hands over the liquid to smell the gases. This is called *wafting*. The children can smell the gas without actually putting their noses on it because the scent of the soda is carried through the air to their noses.

Mystery Bubbles

What happens when air is blown into a liquid?

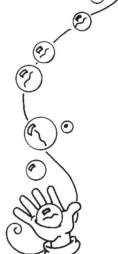

Pour the bubble solution into a clear cup. Have the children help you determine whether the mystery solution is a solid, liquid, or gas. (Because it can be poured, and because it takes the shape of the container that it is in, we know that the mystery solution is a liquid.) Ask the children to guess what the solution is. Pour a small puddle (about 1/8 c. or 30 mL) onto a plastic plate or the table in front of the children. You may let them touch or smell the puddle to get additional clues to the solution's identity.

Have the children predict what they think will happen if you blow air into this liquid? Record the children's ideas and then hand each child a straw. Remind the children to BLOW (not suck) through the straws. As the children blow, they will create familiar objects—bubbles! Now for the trick question: Is a bubble a solid, liquid, or gas? (The outside of the bubble is a liquid and the inside is a gas. If it were a solid, we could touch it and it would not change its shape.)

Science Center: Free Exploration—How can you catch bubbles? Investigate with the children to find out if it is better to use a wet hand (covered with bubble solution) or a dry hand. Ask the children, "How can you measure a bubble?" Allow the children to test their ideas. Be sure to cover the ruler with bubble solution, too.

Mixing It Up

Can I make bubbles in other liquids?

When a gas is mixed into a liquid, it makes a foam known as a *colloid*. Some colloids are wiggly, puffy substances, such as shaving cream and whipped cream, that act a little like liquids and a little like solids. Have the children wash their hands, and then give each child a paper towel. Ask the children to hold out both of their hands. Spray a dollop of whipped topping on one finger of one hand, and place a small spoonful of cream in the palm of the other. Ask the children to compare the two substances. (They are similar, but sugar and air have been added to the whipped topping. The other is just liquid.) Have the children pour the cream and the whipped topping from their hands onto the paper towel. Discuss how the liquid will pour, but not the whipped topping (it may plop). The whipped topping is neither a liquid, nor a solid. If you push it with your finger, it will change shape. Allow the children to try to manipulate the shape of the cream, and taste it if desired.

Have the children help you turn the cream into whipped cream by beating air into it with a handheld electric mixer. (Add sugar as directed on the package.) Now use the same method as above to compare the cream you have whipped to the whipped topping in the can. You have just changed a liquid into "foam."

CROSS-CURRICULAR FUN

Colloid-Mallows Snack

Turn this liquid mixture into a fun, edible science treat by making bubbles in the liquid solution. Follow the directions below.

6 packages unflavored gelatin   3 c. (720 mL) boiling water
3 c. (720 mL) sugar   6 tsp. (30 mL) vanilla
powdered sugar

1. Dissolve unflavored gelatin in boiling water in a mixing bowl. Add sugar and vanilla.
2. Beat with a handheld mixer until the mixture looks airy and creamy like marshmallow crème.
3. Line a baking pan with waxed paper. Spray with cooking spray.
4. Pour the marshmallow mixture into the pan.
5. Cover and let sit overnight.
6. Cut into fun shapes and dust with powdered sugar.
7. Enjoy the colloid-mallows during snack time.

Bubble Art

Cover the bottom of a baking pan with bubble solution. Drop one or two drops of different colored food coloring into the bubble solution. Attach clothespins to the opposite edges of a sheet of copy paper. Using a straw, blow into the bubble solution to make many, many bubbles. While holding the clothespins, quickly and carefully press the paper gently into the bubbles. (Do not push all the way down to the bottom of the pan.) The food coloring will mix with the bubble solution to create a colorful, bubbly work of art on the paper.

LIGHT AND SHADOWS

MATERIALS

- 9 x 12 in. (23 x 30 cm) piece of glass (such as from a picture frame)
- assorted colors of construction paper
- black poster board
- clip-art pictures or coloring book figures
- flashlight
- lightweight cardboard
- masking tape
- opaque and translucent objects for casting shadows
- slide projector or overhead projector
- string
- table and heavy cloth
- tape and scissors
- thin wooden skewers, dowels, or jumbo-sized craft sticks

BOOKS TO SHARE

- *Bear Shadow* by Frank Asch (Simon & Schuster, 1985)
- *Shadow Night* by Kay Chorao (Dutton, 2001)
- *What Makes a Shadow* by Clyde Robert Bulla (HarperCollins, 1994)

Background Information

Young children may have seen shadows on the ground many times while playing outside or walking down a sidewalk. Perhaps they have chased their friends to try to step on their shadows. Exploring how shadows are formed is a great way to relate young children's experiences to science concepts.

Light from the sun and other sources always travels in straight lines. Whenever an object blocks the path of some light rays, a shadow appears. The amount of light that is blocked actually determines how black the shadow is. As children hold an *opaque* object in front of a light source, they will discover that a dark shadow appears because none of the light rays can pass through the object. If a *translucent* object is held in the path of the light, some of the rays are absorbed or blocked while some pass through, creating a shadow that is lighter in intensity. The light rays that are not blocked by the object illuminate the area around the shadow, which makes it possible to see the shape of the shadow.

Objectives

- Observe how objects block light from a light source
- Recognize how the shape of a shadow is related to the shape of the object blocking the light
- Use the body to form shadows on the ground on a sunny day
- Observe how the size of a shadow can be changed
- Record observations using pictures and words
- Explain how shadows are formed

Getting Ready

- Prepare a set of shadow figures by tracing clip-art pictures or mounting coloring-book figures onto black poster board or lightweight cardboard. Trim around the edges and attach each figure to a thin wooden skewer, jumbo-sized craft stick, or dowel with tape. Gather an assortment of figures that are associated with familiar children's stories.

EXPLORATIONS

Now You See It, Now You Don't

What makes a shadow?

Hold up the piece of glass. Ask the children what they think will happen when you shine the light through it. Take several suggestions before demonstrating the outcome. Show this step so the light is shining through the glass at the children, and then also show the results while shining through the glass to a wall. Discuss the outcome. (We can see the light on the other side because the glass is clear.) Ask the children, "What if we shine the light through something that is not clear?" Have the children predict what might happen when you shine a light through the black paper. Test the children's predictions. (This time the light does not go through the paper.) What is different? (The light does not shine through the black paper because it is *opaque*. Opaque objects are solid and block rays of light from passing through them.) Ask, "If I hold different colors of construction paper in front of the light, will the light shine through them?" Test the children's predictions.

Science Center: Free Exploration—Discover what happens when various opaque and translucent objects are held in front of a light source. Provide a "dark area" for the children to work. This can even be the science table covered with a heavy cloth. *Question to investigate:* If a/an [name of translucent object] is held in front of the light, would a dark shadow appear? (Faint shadows will be observed because not all of the light passes through the object.) Allow the children enough time to find out how the shape of the shadow resembles the object blocking the light.

Shadow Play

Why does my shadow follow me?

Take the children outside on a bright, sunny day to observe their shadows. Have them stand in a straight line with their backs to the sun. Ask, "What is similar about all of your shadows? What is different?" Have a child be the leader by creating shadow poses for the other children to match. Continue the game by allowing other children to be leaders.

See if they can make their shadows large or very small. Ask, "How can you make your shadow larger? Can you find a way to make your shadow disappear altogether?" Have the children test their ideas.

Question to investigate: Do the shapes of shadows outdoors change during the day? Have the children test their ideas. Set up the investigation by inserting the dowel for a shadow puppet into the ground. Place a string along the shadow to measure its length. Come back and check the shadow periodically throughout the day.

CROSS-CURRICULAR FUN

Shadow Stories

What does the shape of a shadow tell you?

Large, dark shadows on the wall can be quite fascinating to make and offer wonderful opportunities for children to learn more about the properties of light. Shine a bright light, such as an overhead projector, on a wall. Hold a shadow figure in front of the light so that its shadow can be seen. Ask the children to guess what object the shadow might belong to. Continue with the other shadow figures. *Question to investigate:* If the shadow puppet is held closer to the light source, will the size of its shadow become larger? Have the children test their ideas.

Gather the children around you and share a familiar story with the shadow figures as characters. Have the children help you manipulate the shadows as you retell the story. Alternatively, let the children make up their own shadow stories.

Name _____   Date _____

Take-Home Activity

Shadows Outside

Dear Families,

During science time today, we discovered how shadows are made when light cannot pass through an object. Please help your child do more exploring about shadows by testing different toys and containers outside on a sunny day.

When finished, have your child write or draw a picture about what was discovered on the back of this paper before returning it to school.

Thank you for your assistance,

THE FIVE SENSES

MATERIALS

- cardboard box
- CD player/music
- cotton balls
- cups of water
- food items to sample: pretzels, lemon slices, unsweetened cocoa powder, and chocolate candies
- ingredients and other materials for Molding Dough Creations
- jelly beans
- objects of various textures: pinecones, fuzzy socks, rocks, etc.
- paper bag
- paper hole punch
- paper plate
- snack-sized zippered plastic bags
- various scents and extracts (see preparation notes)
- yarn

BOOKS TO SHARE

- *My Five Senses* by Aliki (HarperTrophy, 1989)
- *Our Senses* by Janine Scott (Compass Point Books, 2003)
- *You Can't Taste a Pickle with Your Ear* by Harriet Ziefert (Blue Apple, 2002)

Background Information

Young children are now discovering how they use specific parts of their bodies known as the sense organs—eyes, ears, nose, tongue, and skin—to learn about different things.

SIGHT: Most of the information that is processed by the brain is acquired by the sense of sight. People use their eyes to "record" details about objects (shapes, sizes, textures, and other properties) and discern distances, movement, and danger. While we look at things, some of the light rays being reflected off the objects travel into our eyes and are focused on the *retinas* as upside-down images. These images are quickly changed into signals and sent to our brains for interpretation. This only happens when there is light to illuminate the objects.

HEAR: The ability to hear sounds is actually quite complex. To produce a sound, something must vibrate, causing sound waves to travel through the air. Some of the sound waves reach the outer ear, move through the ear canal, and then hit the eardrum, making it to vibrate. Those vibrations continue to travel through the middle ear chamber (along three tiny bones) into the *cochlea*, which is located in the inner ear. There the vibrations are converted into nerve impulses and sent to the brain for interpretation. This makes it possible to differentiate between loud and soft sounds, high and low sounds, and pleasant and harsh sounds, as well as to understand speech.

SMELL: The aroma of freshly baked cookies and other odors are actually detected by a special sense organ in the nasal cavity. These sensory nerves known as *olfactory nerves* are sensitive to chemicals floating in the air. As you inhale through your nose, the scent molecules activate special receptors, which send nerve impulses to the brain for interpretation. This sensory organ is quite remarkable because people can distinguish over 3,000 different odors. The sense of smell is also important for keeping our bodies safe, such as detecting spoiled food.

TASTE: The sense of taste is closely linked with the sense of smell. When food is placed in the mouth, food odors also waft into the nostrils and activate those nerve receptors. As the food is chewed, it mixes with saliva and its flavors are detected by *taste buds* located on the upper surface of the tongue. These nerve receptors can differentiate salty, sweet, sour, and bitter tastes.

TOUCH: The sense of touch is important for detecting danger, as well as warmth, coldness, hardness, softness, smoothness, roughness, sharp, dull, vibration, and pressure. Certain receptors in the skin are sensitive to temperature and pain while others detect pressure and motion, such as brushing hair.

Objectives

- Recognize how the five senses are used to collect information
- Discover the importance of the eyes, ears, nose, tongue, and skin

Getting Ready

- Place a cotton ball inside a snack-sized zippered plastic bag for each child. Punch a hole in the top of each bag and loop a 24 in. (61 cm) length of yarn through the hole. Knot the yarn at the ends to create a necklace. Make a necklace for every child and one extra if you have an odd number of children in the class.
- Soak the cotton balls in the bags with a variety of scents, making sure there are two of each scent. Try to use lemon juice, perfume, flavored extracts, vanilla, syrup, and other familiar scents. *Note: Be sure to check for allergies before preparing the materials.*
- Just prior to the lesson, use the punch to make two other holes through the middle of each scent bag.

EXPLORATIONS

Mystery Bag
How do our senses help us identify objects?

Place a small handful of jelly beans in a paper bag. Tell the children that you have a mystery bag and that you want them to use their senses to guess what is inside the bag. Place the mystery bag on the floor in front of you and have the children guess what might be inside. After entertaining a few ideas, tell the children that you are going to give them a clue. Shake the bag and then place it back in front of you. Talk about what sound the items in the bag made. Allow the children to guess again. Next, let the children reach into the bag to feel its contents. Have the children describe what the jelly beans felt like, and then let them make new guesses. Continue by holding the bag so that the children can smell its contents without being able to see what is inside. (You may want to break a couple of jelly beans open for this step.) Have the children describe what they smelled and allow them to continue to guess the contents of the bag. Now have the children close their eyes. Place a jelly bean (*a fresh one that was not in the bag when the children felt its contents*) in each child's mouth. Have them taste the jelly beans and describe them to you. See if the children can identify the jelly beans yet. Finally, allow the children to peek inside the bag and try to identify the jelly beans by sight. Have the children describe what the jelly beans look like.

Scent Partners
How does my nose find a certain scent?

In this game, the children will use their senses of smell and hearing to find partners. Give each child a necklace containing a scented cotton ball. (You will also want to participate if you have an odd number of children in the class.) Have the children move about the room to music. When the music stops, the children stop moving and sniff the necklaces around them to see if the scents match the scents in their own necklaces. Continue dancing and sniffing until everyone finds a partner.

What Do You See?

How do my eyes help me?

To play this game, ask all the children in the room to cover their eyes except for one child who finds a spot to stand. While still covering their eyes, have the children chant to the cadence of "Brown Bear, Brown Bear, what do you see?" inserting the other child's name in place of "Brown Bear." That child then names something that can be seen from where he is standing. Another child in the group tries to guess where the first child might be standing. For example, David chooses a spot by the window. The rest of the class then chants, "David, David, what do you see?" David responds, "I see a blue sky looking at me." One of the children then guesses that David is standing by the window. If the guess is correct, that child chooses another place to stand and the game continues.

Tasty Words

How can I find out which things taste sour, sweet, bitter, or salty?

Place a handful of chocolate candies, a few pretzels, a slice of lemon or sour candy, and a little bit of unsweetened cocoa powder on a paper plate. Also supply each child with a glass of water. To start the activity, have the children taste the pretzels. (The pretzels taste salty.) Have the children take a drink of water and then taste a small amount of cocoa powder. (The powder tastes bitter.) Continue by having the children take a drink and then taste a slice of lemon. (The lemons taste sour.) Finally, direct the children to taste the chocolate candies and describe them. (The candy tastes sweet.) Talk about how our tongues have taste buds for sour, sweet, bitter, and salty flavors. Whenever the taste buds detect a certain flavor, the brain receives the signals that are used for identifying the taste.

Feel Box

How do my fingers help me learn something about objects?

Place an assortment of differently textured objects inside a box that has had a hole cut into one side. Have the children take turns placing one hand inside the box, selecting an item, and then describing the item without naming it. A second child then places a hand in the box to find the described object.

CROSS-CURRICULAR FUN ● ● ● ● ● ●

Molding Dough Creations

- Mix together the following four ingredients in a bowl:
    - 3/4 c. (180 mL) flour
    - 1/3 c. (80 mL) salt
    - 3 tbsp. (45 mL) cornstarch
    - 1 tsp. (5 mL) alum (*sold with spices*)
- Add 1 tsp. (5 mL) of cooking oil and mix thoroughly.
- Add 3/4 c. (180 mL) hot tap water and knead the dough until smooth. (Add food coloring to the water if coloring the dough.) Add a few drops of water if the dough is too dry, and a few drops of flour if it is too sticky.
- Store in a tightly sealed container.

CROSS-CURRICULAR FUN (CONTINUED)

Here are some suggestions for different ways the children can explore with the molding dough before making their creations:

Touch—Add rice, dried peas, sand, clean pebbles, or other items to the dough to change its texture. Create several different textured balls so that the children can compare and contrast the dough through the sense of touch. Alternatively, let the children explore texture independently by adding a variety of substances to their dough. Provide three or four bowls with different materials, such as water, oil, flour, cornstarch, or rice, for the children to use.

Sight—Alter the way the white dough looks by changing its color, or by adding glitter or sequins for a visual effect. Add colors by mixing one or two drops of food coloring into the dough.

Smell—Form several balls of dough, each with a different scent. Add a small spoonful of flavoring, such as orange or peppermint extract, or add scented oils or perfume. Divide each ball of dough in half to see if the children can match the scents, or let them explore independently with their favorite scented dough.

Sound—Ask the children, "What sounds can molding dough produce? What kind of sound is heard when slapping a flat piece of dough against the table? A ball of dough? If you hold the dough close to your ear and pinch it, can you hear a sound? Does the dough sound different when it is cold or warm? Can you trap air bubbles inside the dough and hear them pop when you squish it?" Have the children explore these questions and test their ideas to find out what sounds can be produced by working with molding dough.

After the children have explored how they can alter their molding dough, encourage them to create unusual dough sculptures, which may be displayed in a prominent location.

- -

Name _____   Date _____

Take-Home Activity

The Five Senses

Dear Families,

During science time today, we talked about how we use our five senses. Please help your child do more exploring by observing how foods look, smell, taste, feel, and sound when eating them. Your family may also enjoy playing a guessing game by having everyone try to identify foods using only the sense of smell.

When finished, have your child write or draw a picture about what was discovered on the back of this paper before returning it to school.

Thank you for your assistance,

MY BODY

MATERIALS

- balloons
- cardboard paper-towel tube
- construction paper
- envelopes
- identical blocks
- magnifying glass
- paper
- pattern (page 33)
- picture of human skeleton
- scissors and glue
- slice of bread and milk
- small index cards
- string
- tape
- watercolor markers
- zippered plastic bag
- *Dem Bones* by Bob Barner (Chronicle Books, 1996)
- *Hear Your Heart* by Paul Showers (HarperCollins, 2001)
- *What Happens to a Hamburger?* by Paul Showers (HarperCollins, 2001)

BOOKS TO SHARE

- *A First Book About Bodies* by Nicola Tuxworth (Gareth Stevens Publishing, 1999)
- *From Head to Toe* by Eric Carle (HarperCollins, 1997)
- *Your Skin and Mine* by Paul Showers (HarperTrophy, 1991)

Background Information

During this theme of study, some of the major organs in the human body will be introduced to the children.

SKIN: The skin is an amazing organ because it protects everything inside the body from bumps and bruises and germs, while also keeping the major organs clean. It prevents water from entering so we can take baths and showers. Each month new skin cells are made, keeping that protective layer strong.

BONES: These marvelous hard substances comprise the framework that not only gives the body shape but also protects important organs like the heart, lungs, and brain. Bones cannot move independently. Skeletal muscles, which also give the body shape, make it possible for bones to be moved at the joints by contracting and relaxing. For example, the biceps muscle in the upper arm pulls the arm up toward the body (bending the elbow) while the triceps muscle relaxes. When you want to straighten your arm, the triceps muscle contracts while the biceps muscle relaxes.

The bones in the body have different shapes and are built to withstand strains and stresses as you move in various ways. There are long, strong bones with straight shafts that make up the arms (*humerus, ulna,* and *radius*) and legs (*femur, tibia,* and *fibula*). Short bones with central shafts are found in the hands (palm— *metacarpals*), fingers (*phalanges*), feet (*metatarsals*), and toes (*phalanges*). Small irregular-shaped bones comprise the wrists (*carpals*) and ankles (*tarsals*). Various-shaped bones also make up the skull (*cranium*), shoulder blades (*scapula*), breastbone (*sternum*), hip (*pelvis*), collarbone (*clavicle*), and ribs. The odd-shaped bones in the spine (*vertebrae*) support the weight of the body while sitting and standing.

In certain parts of the body, the ends of bones meet other bones to form joints, making it possible for a person to move in different ways. For example, knees, elbows, and fingers are called *hinge joints* and can move back and forth. There are also *ball-and-socket joints* in the hips and shoulders that allow legs and arms to rotate and move in almost any direction.

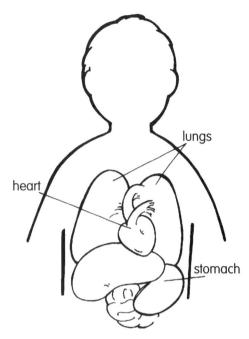

labels: lungs, heart, stomach

HEART: Working nonstop, the *heart* is a pump that forces blood to flow throughout the body. The walls of the heart, known as *cardiac muscles*, are different from the muscles that move bones. The heart is actually two pumps working simultaneously side by side. The right pump sends blood that has returned from cells throughout the body to the lungs. When the blood carrying a fresh supply of oxygen returns from the lungs, it travels through the left chambers of the heart and then out into strong, stretchy tubes called *arteries*. These specialized tubes assist in carrying the blood to different parts of the body by expanding and contracting, forcing the blood cells to move forward to maintain blood pressure. The work is constant as the heart continually pumps blood into the tubes. The marvelous network of arteries, veins, and capillaries provides the "roadways" for blood to travel to and from all cells in the body.

LUNGS: Inside the chest cavity are two elastic-like bags called *lungs* that expand as air is inhaled by the body. Within the right lung and the left lung, oxygen passes through very thin walls of air sacs to reach the blood. Simultaneously, carbon dioxide moves from the blood through the walls into the air sacs and is later carried out of the body when a person exhales. How frequently a person needs to breathe depends on how active the body is. When you sleep, your breathing rate is slow and shallow. This is quite different from when you are running. Then you need to take frequent deep breaths because your body is expending more energy.

STOMACH AND INTESTINES: The stomach and intestines are part of the digestive system. The job of the digestive system is to break down food into very small particles. This process starts in the mouth, where the teeth chop and grind the food as it is mixed with saliva to make it soft. Then the tongue slides the food into the throat for swallowing.

The soft, chewed food travels down a tube called the *esophagus* and enters the *stomach*. This sack-like organ continues the job of breaking down the food by squishing and mashing it while strong digestive fluids act on it. This process of digestion continues as the food moves through the *small intestine*. When the food particles are completely digested, they are small enough to pass through the walls of the small intestine into the bloodstream. Then they are transported to various cells and burned as energy when the cells do their work. Waste products from the digestion of foods travel into the *large intestine* and are later eliminated from the body.

Objectives

• Recognize the importance of the skin, bones, heart, lungs, stomach, intestines, and brain
• Identify where the heart, lungs, stomach, and bones are located in the body

Getting Ready

• Make a copy of the Build-A-Body pattern on page 33. Color as desired and cut along the dashed lines to separate the pieces. Tape each piece onto the side of a wooden building block.
• Cut five 12 in. (30 cm) lengths of string for the set of blocks. Tape one end of each string to the back side of each block prepared with the Build-A-Body pattern page as previously mentioned.
• Make a copy of the pattern page for each child. If appropriate, cut out the pieces and store them in an envelope for each child.
• Inflate a small balloon for each child.

EXPLORATIONS ● ● ● ● ● ● ● ● ● ● ●

Every Part Is Important

Which body parts are important?

Ask the children to imagine making a peanut butter sandwich without the bread or peanut butter. It would not be a very good sandwich, would it? Every part of the sandwich is important.

Just like a peanut butter sandwich, all parts of our bodies are important. Have the children name as many body parts as they can. Choose one child to come up and help you. As the children name different body parts, record the name of each one on an index card and then tape the card onto the designated child's body. Discuss why each part is important. Have all the children point to or move their corresponding body parts. For example, if "knees" were suggested, your helper would place the card on his knee and then you would comment about how our knees help us walk and climb up and down stairs.

Building Blocks   *Which body parts are necessary?*

Have the children help you stack the blocks with the build-a-body pictures in order starting with the feet. Tell the children that this tower of blocks is just like them. Every part is important, and if something is not working right, the whole tower (or our whole body) could come tumbling down. Demonstrate by telling the children that if your heart stops working (pull out the block for the chest by tugging on the string) your whole body stops working.

Build-A-Body   *What are the parts of the body?*

Give each child a sheet of construction paper and a set of Build-A-Body pieces. Have the children put the parts in order to build the body. Then glue the strips onto construction paper and color as desired. So what are these important parts? Have the children do the following activities to explore a few of the important parts of their bodies:

• **Skin**—Have the children feel their skin. Some skin (like on our arms) is rougher than other skin (behind our ears). Skin holds everything in, and it protects everything inside by keeping the good stuff (blood) in and the bad stuff (germs) out. Take a close look at skin using a magnifying glass. Alternatively, read aloud parts of the book *Your Skin and Mine* by Paul Showers (HarperTrophy, 1991) to the children.
• **Bones**—Show a lifelike skeleton or a picture of one and have the children locate the corresponding bones on their bodies as you point to them on the skeleton. As you discuss certain bones, have the children feel their own bones. Some are big and some are very little. The skull, ribs, elbows, kneecaps, spine, and fingers are the easiest bones to feel. If appropriate for the children, play "Head, Shoulders, Knees and Toes" substituting the names of bones as you sing. Alternatively, read aloud the book *Dem Bones* by Bob Barner and enjoy singing that song with the children.

EXPLORATIONS (CONTINUED)

- **Heart**—The heart is actually a muscle that pumps blood throughout our bodies. Have each child make a fist and then open the hand, repeating this motion until the hand feels tired. Compare this motion with what the heart does without stopping. Give each child an inflated balloon to squish rhythmically. Discuss with the children how the heart works. It pumps the blood out to other parts of the body. Continue the lesson by reading aloud parts of the book *Hear Your Heart* by Paul Showers and then have the children use a paper-towel tube as a stethoscope to listen for heartbeats.
- **Lungs**—Show the children two slightly inflated balloons. Explain how this is what the lungs look like before a person takes a breath. Have everyone take a deep breath and feel their chests expanding. As they breathe in, inflate the balloons. Talk about how the lungs transfer oxygen to the blood.
- **Stomach and Intestines**—Our tummies hold food and get it ready to send to the small intestine. Show the children the zippered plastic bag. Place a piece of bread and some milk in the bag, and seal the bag tightly. Squish the contents together to demonstrate how the stomach works. Explain that when you hear your tummy "growl," it is just your tummy at work, breaking down the food into small parts. It can take several hours before the food moves into the small intestine. There the digestion continues until the food parts are tiny enough to be carried by the blood to cells in every part of the body. Have each child lay an ear on another child's tummy and listen to the growling, gurgling noises of the digestive system. If the children are interested, read aloud parts of the book *What Happens to a Hamburger?* by Paul Showers to learn more about these organs.
- **Brain**—Hold up a blank sheet of paper. This is what we would see, feel, taste, smell, etc., if our brains did not work. Our brains take experiences and turn them into thoughts or information. For example, when our eyes record a house (draw a house on the paper), our brains tell us what it is.

  After introducing these main body parts, generate a list of ways to take good care of our bodies and record the children's ideas on chart paper. Suggestions might include playing safe so we do not injure ourselves, getting enough sleep so our bodies can grow, eating healthful foods, playing active games, exercising, and getting rest when we are sick.

CROSS-CURRICULAR FUN

Can You Do This?

Have the children list movements that their bodies can do, such as run, jump, and bend. Discuss why it is possible for their bodies to be flexible. Continue the lesson by having the children try to move their bodies in certain ways that are hard, harder, or even impossible. Some ideas to consider:

- Join your hands behind your back.
- Bend over and hold your ankles while trying to jump forward.
- Kiss your elbow.
- Stick your elbow in your ear.
- Squat down low and then stand back up.
- Lie on the ground and pull one leg all the way up to your head.

Build-A-Body Pattern

DAY AND NIGHT

MATERIALS

- 2 cardboard boxes
- construction paper
- crayons
- flashlight
- globe
- large garbage bag or container
- masking tape
- objects seen in daytime
- objects seen in nighttime
- paper stars and moon
- patterns (page 37)
- pictures of daytime sky
- pictures of nighttime sky
- scissors and glue
- watercolor markers
- *Owl Moon* by Jane Yolen (Philomel, 1987)

BOOKS TO SHARE

- *Day and Night* by Maria Gordon (Thomson Learning, 1995)
- *Where Are the Night Animals?* by Mary Ann Fraser (HarperTrophy, 1999)

Background Information

The sun is the source of light and heat for Earth. It is difficult for children to understand that even though the sun appears to travel across the sky, this change in position is actually due to Earth's rotation. Point out to the children that the amount of daylight increases during the late winter and spring seasons and shortens during the late summer and fall seasons.

Objectives

- Identify objects that are representative either of daytime events or of nighttime events
- Describe objects seen in the nighttime sky (moon and stars)
- Describe objects seen in the daytime sky (sun, moon, aircraft)
- Observe and compare daytime and nighttime skies
- Identify the sun as the source of light and heat for Earth

Getting Ready

- Using watercolor markers, draw a large sun on the front of one box and a picture of a nighttime sky on the other box.
- Gather a selection of objects that represent daytime events and other objects for nighttime events. Ideas might include the following items: daytime—lunchbox, picture of daytime sky, ball, and clothing; and nighttime—pajamas, flashlight, pillow, and pictures of the moon and stars. Make sure you have at least one object per child. Place the objects in a large garbage bag.
- If desired, send home a note requesting that the children bring pillows and wear their pajamas on the day you plan to discuss the concepts of day and night.
- Tape pictures of the moon and stars randomly on the ceiling and the picture of the owl on page 37 on a wall.
- Make a copy of the daytime/nighttime pictures for each child.

EXPLORATIONS • • • • • • • • •

Day and Night
How do we know when it is daytime?

Ask the children, "How do we know when it is daytime?" Allow the children to answer and then ask how they know when it is nighttime. (The sun and other celestial objects such as stars and the moon help us to know if it is daytime or nighttime. When the sun comes up above the horizon in the morning, its light is scattered over the earth. It *appears to travel* across the sky during the day and sets in the west in the evening.) Go outside and note where the sun is located in the sky. *Be sure to remind the children not to look directly at the sun.* If possible, mark its position in relation to some other physical object, such as a tree or building. Throughout the day, take time to check outside for the location of the sun. At the end of the day, talk about how the sun appears low in the sky in the morning and seems to move across the opposite part of the sky until it sets on the western horizon. Remind the children to look for the sun when they eat dinner in the evening, and again in the morning when they wake up.

Science Center: Free Exploration—If appropriate, provide a globe and flashlight ("the sun") for the children to use to demonstrate how one side of Earth receives light from the sun during daylight hours while it is nighttime on the other side of Earth.

Daytime/Nighttime Sorting Fun

What objects do we use specifically during daytime? During nighttime?

Select one object from the bag of daytime/nighttime objects. Hold it up for all the children to see and identify. Ask the children to tell you whether it is an object to use in the daytime or in the nighttime. Once the object has been identified, ask the children to think if the object ever could be used at another time of day. For example, if you pull out a pair of pajamas, the children would identify them as a nighttime object, but there may be circumstances (perhaps during an illness) when the pajamas could also be used during the day. Have the children take turns selecting objects, identifying them, and classifying them as daytime or nighttime objects.

CROSS-CURRICULAR FUN • • • • • • •

Good Night, Sun

Choose one of the children's daytime activities, such as running or jumping, and have all the children act out that activity. Ask, "What sounds can you hear?" Direct the children to sit quietly and listen for daytime sounds. They might hear children on the playground, cars on the road, or birds singing.

Now have the children get their pillows and curl up on the floor for a bedtime story. Turn out the lights and read *Owl Moon* by Jane Yolen. Have the children lie very still and listen for any nighttime sounds. Imagine listening to crickets or an owl hooting in the distance. Turn on the flashlight and look for stars in the sky. Remind the children to whisper quietly so they will not scare off the owl. Find the owl (picture) with the flashlight and imagine it flying away.

Talk about how *nocturnal* animals are active at night. Animals that are active during the daytime are known as *diurnal* animals. Alternatively, read aloud the book *Where Are the Night Animals?* by Mary Ann Fraser (HarperTrophy, 1999).

CROSS-CURRICULAR FUN (CONTINUED)

Daytime and Nighttime Book

To help children think about their favorite daytime and nighttime activities, you might consider making a class book. First, provide each child with a copy of the Daytime/Nighttime pictures (page 37). Color, cut out, and glue each image onto a large sheet of construction paper that has been divided in half. Now the children can write about or draw pictures of favorite things to do during daytime and nighttime hours. When the pages are finished, collate them into a large book for the chidren to "read."

Alternatively, make a list of the best things to do during the daytime by having the children tell you about their favorite activities. Write their ideas on a piece of poster board and label it with the picture of the sun and the word "Daytime." Repeat the activity for nighttime or late evening activities when you can see the moon and stars in the sky.

✂ --

Name _____   Date _____

Take-Home Activity

Looking at the Night Sky

Dear Families,

During science time today, we talked about day and night. Please help your child learn more about things that can be seen in the night sky. Would you and your child spend a few minutes late in the evening looking at the moon and the stars sometime during this week? Be sure to talk about the shape of the moon and how it will change.

When finished, have your child write or draw a picture about what was discovered on the back of this paper before returning it to school.

Thank you for your assistance,

Picture Patterns

Daytime

Nighttime

WATCHING THE WEATHER

MATERIALS

- black or dark-colored construction paper
- flour and plate
- index cards
- paintbrushes
- paper brads
- paper plates
- patterns (page 41)
- plastic grocery sacks
- salt and water
- scissors and glue
- snow or ice shavings
- sticks and string
- student thermometer
- watercolor markers
- *What Will the Weather Be Like Today?* by Paul Rogers (Scholastic, 1997)

BOOKS TO SHARE

- *Clouds* by Maryellen Gregoire (Bridgestone Books, 2005)
- *Gilberto and the Wind* by Marie Hall Ets (Puffin, 1978)
- *Hello, Sun!* by Dayle Ann Dodds (Dial, 2005)
- *Rain Talk* by Mary Serfozo (McElderry Books, 1990)
- *The Snowy Day* by Ezra Jack Keats (Puffin, 1978)
- *What Will the Weather Be?* by Lynda DeWitt (HarperCollins, 1991)

Background Information

What makes the weather change? Weather is created by the movement of large air masses and their pressures, the amount of heat energy in the atmosphere, and the amount of moisture in the air. The sun fuels the energy for heating the earth's surface. As the ground warms, some of that heat energy is transferred back into the layer of air that is closest to the ground by a process called *conduction*. After the air becomes warmer, it rises up into the atmosphere (a process called *convection*) and is replaced by cooler air. These rising air currents are known as *thermals*. This cycle is continuous as sunshine heats the ground, buildings, and pavement on streets. Green plants and trees also play a critical role in this cycle because their thin leaves quickly conduct the heat back into the surrounding air to prevent becoming overheated. Clouds will form in the atmosphere when warm, moist air meets cold air and cools. The amount of moisture in the clouds will impact how heavy a rain shower might be. When rain falls through cold air, it freezes and turns into sleet. If moisture is carried up high in the clouds and freezes, then snowflakes or hail might be formed, depending on the conditions. Scientists called *meteorologists* study changing air conditions (temperature, humidity, wind, and air pressure) to predict the weather.

If you would like additonal information about weather, locate a good resource book. For example, *The Kids' Book of Clouds & Sky* by Frank Staub (Sterling Publishing, 2003) is an excellent source of information for questions that children might ask about weather. The photographs are fascinating for children to look at, too!

Objectives

- Observe how the warmth of the sun causes water to evaporate, leaving salt crystals behind on black paper
- Observe how the wind moves objects
- Recognize the direction of the wind by watching a wind sock
- Observe how warm air temperatures affect the liquid in a thermometer, causing it to rise
- Recognize that very cold air temperatures cause water to freeze
- Predict what the weather conditions will be like later in the day

Getting Ready

- Prepare salt water by dissolving salt in very warm tap water.
- Make a sample weather wheel with a copy of the pictures depicting weather conditions on page 41. Color, cut out, and glue the pictures onto a paper plate to create a weather wheel. Make a copy of the weather pictures for each child.

EXPLORATIONS

Observing the Weather
Can you tell what the weather will be?

Weather permitting, go outside and have everyone lie on their backs in a circle with their heads in the center. Look at the sky, and talk about clouds and the air temperature. Read aloud the book *What Will the Weather Be Like Today?* by Paul Rogers (Scholastic, 1997). Discuss the different kinds of weather, and ask the children to predict what they think the weather will be like later in the day.

A Sunny Day at Work
If salt water is left in the warm sunshine, what will happen to it?

Energy from the sun warms up the air. This is why it feels hot when we go outside in the summer. Even when it is cloudy outside, some of the energy from the sun is warming the ground and air.

Watch the sun at work. Have the children paint salt water on pieces of black or dark-colored construction paper. Set the papers in a sunny spot and hold them in place by using a weight, such as a rock. After a few hours, note how the water has evaporated and the paper is now dry. Discuss with the children how the heat from the sun evaporates the water but not the salt that is left behind.

Shopping-Bag Wind Sock
How can you tell which direction the wind is blowing?

Investigate with the children how the wind moves objects outside. Ask, "How could you know if there was a gentle breeze without actually feeling it?" Have the children test their ideas by watching leaves on trees. Continue the lesson by intoducing the children to wind socks. Gather a 24 in. (61 cm) stick for each child. Help the children tie a plastic shopping bag to each stick with a string. Push the sticks into the ground. Observe the wind socks throughout the day and the week to determine the direction of the wind. If the plastic bags are floating toward the north, the wind is blowing from the south. Keep a log of the direction of the wind.

Raindrop Catcher
What does a raindrop look like?

On a rainy day, stick your hand out the window, or out from under an awning or umbrella to "catch" a raindrop. Note how the raindrop crashes and spreads all over your hand. Now try catching a raindrop in a plate of flour. Ask, "Did the raindrop splatter? Did it form a small ball?" Alternatively, continue the experiment trying different substances, such as cornstarch, sugar, and salt, to see which one makes the best raindrop catcher.

Weather Wheel   *What will the weather be like this afternoon?*

To make the weather wheel, give each child a paper plate and a copy of the weather pictures on page 41. Use only the pictures that show sky conditions, wind, and precipitation. Have the children color the pictures and then cut out and glue each one onto their paper plates. Next, have them draw and cut out arrows, using index cards. Attach the arrows to their paper plates with paper brads.

Use the weather wheels when observing and predicting the weather. For example, in the morning have each child make a prediction about the weather conditions later in the day and then point the arrow on the weather wheel toward the corresponding picture. Check the wheels later in the day to see whose predictions were accurate.

Measuring the Air Temperature   *How warm is the air?*

Find a large thermometer for the children to view. At the same time each day, read the thermometer and use a piece of tape to mark the temperature reading. Encourage the children to observe how the temperature changes or stays about the same each day. *Note: It is not important for young children to be able to read the thermometer. Instead, they should start to observe that a higher temperature means warmer air and so on.* The measurements can be displayed on a simple bar graph to help the children see the relationship between heat and air temperature. Choose one of the pictures of children wearing different garments (on page 41) to best represent the air temperature outside and attach it near the graph.

Melting Snow   *What happens to snow when it gets warm?*

Capture some snowflakes (or sprinkle shaved ice) on a sheet of black construction paper. Ask, "What will happen to snow if it is brought into the classroom?" Take your captured snowflakes indoors and watch what happens. Discuss how snow is simply rain that gets frozen and automatically returns to water droplets when it is warm. Have the children think of ways to keep their snowflakes frozen.

CROSS-CURRICULAR FUN ● ● ● ● ● ●

Weather Song

Sing to the tune of "If You're Happy and You Know It."

If it's sunny and you know it, clap your hands.
If it's cloudy and you know it, stomp your feet.
If it's rainy and you know it, then the weather will surely show it.
If it's snowy and you know it, rub your tummy.

Alternatively, repeat the song, inserting the type of weather you are currently experiencing. For example, if the weather is sunny, sing the song by replacing all of the other weather words with "sunny" as indicated: "If it's sunny and you know it, clap your hands. If it's sunny and you know it, stomp your feet. . . ."

Weather Pictures and Dressing for the Weather Patterns

BUGS AND OTHER INSECTS

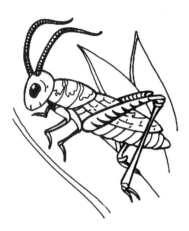

MATERIALS

- baby food jars or plastic containers
- chenille stems
- crayons or markers
- insects
- magnifying glass
- mirror
- paper plates
- patterns (pages 45-46)
- paper hole punch
- scissors and glue
- stapler
- string

BOOKS TO SHARE

- *Bug Safari* by Bob Barner (Holiday House, 2004)
- *Bugs Are Insects* by Anne Rockwell (HarperCollins, 2001)
- *Hungry Hoppers: Grasshoppers in Your Backyard* by Nancy Loewen (Picture Window Books, 2004)
- *Insects* by Melissa Steward (Children's Press, 2001)

Background Information

What is an insect? An insect is an invertebrate that has three main body parts known as the head, thorax, and abdomen; six legs (three pairs) for jumping, walking, and/or balance; two antennae for sensing and tasting; and an exoskeleton. Not all insects have wings, so this trait is not a main characteristic.

Many adult insects use their legs basically for walking and keeping their balance, while others have more specialized features. Grasshoppers have strong, large back legs for leaping and jumping. Flies have tiny suction cups on their feet to help them stick to surfaces making it possible to walk up walls or even upside down. Water striders use their tiny feet and long legs to skate on top of water in ponds. Bees have special pouches on their legs for carrying food.

Insects eat everything from leaves to other insects, but they do not have teeth like humans. Instead, they have different kinds of mouthparts. The butterfly has a long, straw-like mouthpart called a *proboscis*. It uses the proboscis like a straw to suck up nectar from flowers. Grasshoppers use their jagged jaws for cutting off small parts of leaves. Mosquitoes have long, spear-like mouthparts that they poke into people or other animals.

If you would like to learn more about insects, locate a good reference book. For example, *Everything Bug: What Kids Really Want to Know About Insects and Spiders* by Cherie Winner (NorthWord Press, 2004) offers a lot of useful information.

Objectives

- Recognize an insect by its three main body parts and three pairs of legs
- Observe how insects move by walking, flying, or jumping
- Identify different mouthparts of insects

Getting Ready

- Several days before beginning this activity, collect live and dead insects around the school. If possible, collect one insect for each child to observe or invite children to help out by bringing insects they have collected that are not dangerous to school. Keep each bug in a separate baby food jar or large plastic container with airholes. *Note: Direct young children not to pick up insects unless an adult has given them permission. It is important to inform children about insects that sting or bite.*
- Make copies of the patterns on pages 45 and 46 for each child.

EXPLORATIONS ● ● ● ● ● ● ● ●

Looking at Insects   *What is an insect?*

Give each child a jar with a bug inside. Have the children look carefully at their bugs and then ask them to think about what all of these animals have in common. List the children's ideas on chart paper. (Some insects do not have wings. Some do not have eyes. However, all insects have an exoskeleton that covers their three main body parts and three pairs of legs.) Discuss how insects do not have bones. Have the children feel the bones on the insides of their own arms. Talk about how all of our bones together make up our skeletons. Explain that insects have hard outer shells called *exoskeletons*. An insect's exoskeleton is not as hard as a person's skeleton. (This is why insects squish so easily.) Continue the lesson by comparing the insects' bodies, looking for similarities or differences in color, size, and shape. Also look for specific markings, such as bright colors and spots, or specialized adaptations, such as a double set of wings, extra-armored bodies, and so on.

Extend the lesson by reading aloud the book *Bugs Are Insects* by Anne Rockwell to help children understand the difference between insects and other creepy-crawly bugs, such as spiders and centipedes.

Bugs on the Move   *Why do insects need six legs?*

How do insects move? Have the children take a look at their own legs and then study the legs of the insects they are observing. Ask, "How are the legs of insects different than yours? Can you jump like a grasshopper? Can you walk up a wall like a fly?" Discuss and record the children's observations on chart paper.

Where Are the Teeth?   *How do bugs eat?*

Have the children look at their own teeth in a mirror. Talk about how their front teeth are thin and flat, and can be used for biting and tearing food. Point out how they chew and grind their food with the big, bumpy teeth (molars) in the back of their mouths. Now use a magnifying glass to look at the mouths of your insects. *Question to investigate:* How can you find out what kinds of food the insect eats? Allow children to test their ideas.

CROSS-CURRICULAR FUN ● ● ● ● ● ● ●

Bug Hats

1. Look at the pattern pages. Choose one of the heads for the hat and then color and cut out the pieces.
2. Cut out the middle of a paper plate, leaving a 1 1/2 in. (38 mm) rim around the outer edge.
3. Punch four holes on each side of the paper-plate rim.
4. Glue the head of the insect to the paper-plate rim (see the illustration on this page). Attach the antennae to the head.
5. Glue the abdomen to the opposite side of the paper plate and add wings, if desired, by attaching pieces of tissue paper.
6. To make the legs, thread a chenille stem through each of three holes on each side of the rim. Twist to secure the six legs.
7. Tie a 12 in. (30 cm) length of string in the remaining hole on each side of the "thorax."
8. Place the hat on the head and secure by tying the ends of the string.

CROSS-CURRICULAR FUN (CONTINUED) ● ● ● ● ● ●

Insects Olympics

Everyone can wear their bug hats while participating in these fun activities:

- **Grasshopper Hop**—Mark a starting line and see how far you can jump.
- **Mosquito Sip**—Use a drinking straw for a proboscis. Pick up a 1 in. (25 mm) square piece of paper with the straw and carefully carry it home to the starting line.
- **Dung Beetle Roll**—Dung beetles roll dung (elephant poop) around to create large balls and then use them for nests for their babies. Mark a line on one side of the playground. Roll a ball to the other side of the playground using only your nose.
- **Ant Life**—Ants are very strong and can lift many times their own weight. Grab a block or toy and lift it high over your head. Continue lifting and counting until you feel tired.
- **Inchworm Races**—Travel from one side of the playground to the other by moving like an inchworm. After positioning your hands and feet on the ground, crawl forward on your hands only. Now walk with your feet forward until they meet up with your hands. Repeat the process until you have crossed the finish line!

✂ -

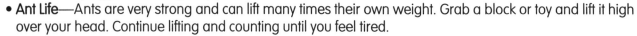

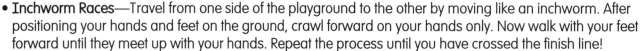

Name _____   Date _____

Take-Home Activity

Looking at Insects

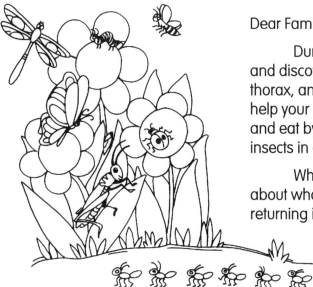

Dear Families,

During science time today, we talked about insects and discovered that they have three distinct body parts (head, thorax, and abdomen) and six legs (three pairs). Please help your child do more exploring about how insects move and eat by watching those that do not sting or bite. Look for insects in a garden, your backyard, or a nearby park.

When finished, have your child write or draw a picture about what was discovered on the back of this paper before returning it to school.

Thank you for your assistance,

Bug Hat Pattern

(Heads)

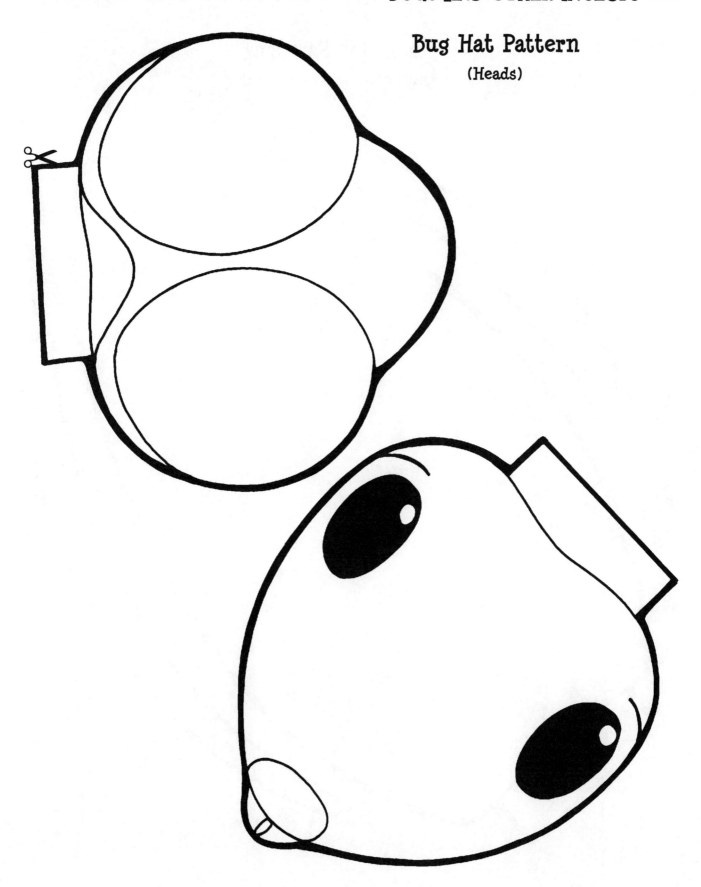

Bug Hat Pattern
(Antennae and Abdomen)

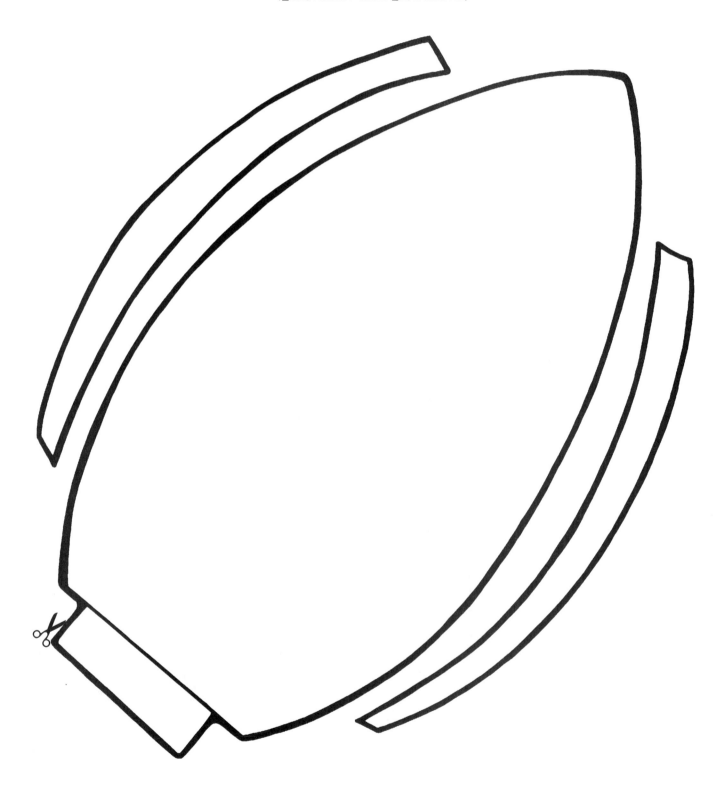

46

WATCHING CATERPILLARS

MATERIALS

- caterpillars
- cheesecloth
- chenille stems
- craft sticks
- empty cardboard box
- fresh leaves
- large, empty plastic containers
- magnifying glasses
- paper and stapler
- patterns (page 50)
- roll cotton-quilt batting
- scissors and glue
- tissue paper
- toilet-paper tubes
- watercolor markers
- *Caterpillars* by Patrick Merrick (The Child's World, Inc., 1988)
- *The Very Hungry Caterpillar* by Eric Carle (Philomel, 1981)

BOOKS TO SHARE

- *Butterfly House* by Eve Bunting (Scholastic, 1999)
- *From Caterpillar to Butterfly* by Deborah Heiligman (HarperTrophy, 1996)
- *Night Fliers: Moths in Your Backyard* by Nancy Loewen (Picture Window Books, 2004)
- *Waiting for Wings* by Lois Ehlert (Harcourt, 2001)

Background Information

All butterfly and moth caterpillars are born by hatching from eggs and then quickly proceed to eat their first meals—their own eggshells. As the caterpillar, or *larva*, feeds on plant leaves, its body grows and becomes too large for its outer body casing. When a new casing has grown under the outer casing, the caterpillar will take in air to inflate itself, causing the old casing to burst open down the middle of the back. Then the caterpillar crawls out of the old "skin." This cycle of eating, growing, and molting happens four to six times until the insect becomes a mature caterpillar.

The mature caterpillar stops growing and enters the *pupal*, or resting stage of its life cycle. Its body starts to change. If the caterpillar will become an adult butterfly, it attaches one end of its body to a plant stem or twig and then hangs down in a familiar "J" shape. Its hard outer case falls off, revealing the pupal case, or *chrysalis*. If the caterpillar will become an adult moth, it may spin some kind of cocoon, hide in dead leaves or grass to cover its pupal case, or burrow into the ground. Inside each pupal case, an incredible transformation takes place: the wormlike caterpillar changes into a body with three distinct parts, three pairs of legs, and two pairs of wings covered with tiny scales.

Objectives

- Observe how caterpillars feed on leaves
- Identify traits that different kinds of caterpillars have in common
- Observe how caterpillars change into butterflies or moths
- Record how caterpillars for moths and butterflies differ

Getting Ready

- Make copies of the letter to families on page 49 and send them home with the children a few days prior to doing this theme. Invite the children to search for caterpillars that could be brought to school for observation.
- Make a copy of the butterfly and caterpillar on page 50. Color them as desired and then cut out the finished figures. Cover a cardboard cereal box with colored paper. Glue the caterpillar on one side of the box and the butterfly on the other side.
- Create a mini-habitat for each caterpillar out of a large, clear plastic container, such as a pretzel container. Provide fresh plant leaves that the caterpillar prefers to eat. If possible, identify which kind of caterpillar it is and then feed it accordingly. Keep the caterpillar away from direct sunlight and wash the container every few days. Cover the opening of the jar with cheesecloth that has been secured with a rubber band.

EXPLORATIONS · · · · · · · · · · ·

Life Cycles
How do caterpillars change into butterflies?

All insects change during their lifetimes. They are born by hatching from eggs, they eat, they grow and shed their outer shells several times, and eventually, they die. This is what happens to insects like crickets, grasshoppers, katydids, and others that resemble their parents when they are born. Other insects, such as butterflies and moths, actually have four distinct stages in their life cycles: egg, larva (caterpillar), pupa, and adult. When caterpillars transform into butterflies during the pupa stage, this change is called *metamorphosis*. Read aloud the book *The Very Hungry Caterpillar* (Philomel, 1981), using the caterpillar box as a prop. At the appropriate time, wrap the box with cotton-quilt batting. When it is time to reveal the butterfly, turn the box around as you unwrap it.

Caterpillar Observations
What does a caterpillar do all day?

Even though caterpillars move slowly, they are fascinating animals to watch. After reading the book *The Very Hungry Caterpillar*, discuss how all caterpillars eat only leaves, not many of the foods featured in the story. In fact, some kinds of caterpillars are actually very picky eaters, feeding only on specific kinds of leaves. For example, the monarch caterpillar munches only on milkweed plant leaves. The cabbage caterpillar prefers leaves on cabbage, broccoli, and cauliflower plants. For large, clear pictures and additional information about caterpillars, read aloud the book *Caterpillars* by Patrick Merrick (The Child's World, Inc., 1988) to the children.

Ask the children, "How can we find out what a caterpillar likes to eat?" Record their ideas on chart paper. Place each of the caterpillars along with the leaves the children have collected in a shallow tin pie plate. Provide magnifying lenses for the children to use when observing the caterpillars. Encourage the children to watch the caterpillars eating food or observe evidence that they have been eating. (Their droppings are called *frass*.) Be sure to ask questions about how the caterpillars move and how their bodies are similar or different from others. As a group, create a Caterpillar Observation Chart that lists and answers the following questions:

- *How do caterpillars move?*
- *How do caterpillars eat?*
- *How do caterpillars grow?*
- *How are the caterpillars different? The same?*

If interested, have the children draw pictures of their caterpillars on the chart before hanging it in a prominent spot in the classroom.

Return the caterpillars to their mini-habitats. Continue to observe the caterpillars throughout the day. Before closing for the end of the school day, talk again with the children about their observations. See if they have anything new to add or if further observations have changed their ideas about caterpillars. Send the children home with the caterpillars to release them in the same locations where they were found so each one can find the food it needs.

Science Center: Free Exploration—Consider extending the lesson by contacting *www.butterflynursery. com* to purchase caterpillar larvae for the children to observe changing into butterflies. Having a special place outdoors to observe butterflies is also an effective way to connect children with nature. If interested, think about building a small, butterfly-friendly garden by researching which plants attract butterflies and will grow well in your area. Plants to consider include asters, black-eyed Susans, coreopsis, cosmos, liatris, marigolds, parsley, phlox, purple coneflowers, and zinnias. After obtaining permission from your school's administration, create a small garden by planting flowers in the ground or large containers.

Alternatively, collect caterpillars, identify them, and provide a safe habitat in large, clear plastic containers so the children can watch the caterpillars change into butterflies or moths.

CROSS-CURRICULAR FUN • • • • • •

Hungry Caterpillars

Have the children create their own "Very Hungry Caterpillars." Provide copies of the patterns on page 50 for the children to use. Give each child an empty toilet-paper tube to decorate as desired with crayons or markers. Color, cut out, and glue the caterpillar onto the tube. Punch two holes in the tube and head of the caterpillar. Thread a chenille stem through the holes, twisting the ends on the outside of the tube to create antennae. Using the butterfly pattern as a guide, cut a piece of tissue paper into a butterfly shape. Glue a craft stick to the middle of the tissue butterfly. Roll the butterfly around the craft stick and insert it into the middle of the caterpillar tube. Invite the children to tell their own stories about caterpillars. At the appropriate time, have the child pull out the craft stick to make the butterfly emerge from the tube.

Butterfly Journal

Children will enjoy writing and drawing pictures about butterflies in these special journals! To make the journals, photocopy the butterfly pattern on page 50 for each child. Have the children color their butterflies as desired. Place the butterfly shape on top of a few sheets of paper. Staple the pages together and then cut around the outline of the butterfly through the layers of paper to make a butterfly-shaped booklet.

✂ -

• •

Name _____   Date _____

Take-Home Activity

Watching Caterpillars

Dear Families,

During science time today, we talked about young butterflies and moths and discovered that they are called caterpillars. Please help your child search for a caterpillar that could be brought to school. When you find a caterpillar, note what kind of leaves it is eating and gather a few of those, too. Place the caterpillar and the leaves in a clean, plastic container and punch some airholes in the lid.

When we are finished watching the caterpillar, please return it to the same location where it was found.

Thank you for your assistance,

Butterfly and Caterpillar Patterns

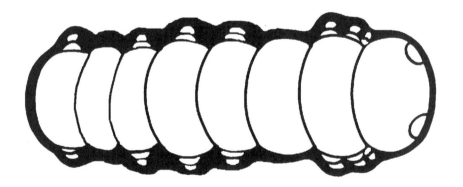

GROWING PLANTS

MATERIALS

- 4 identical plants
- assortment of fresh vegetable produce with leaves and roots intact
- clear plastic cups
- jumbo-sized craft sticks
- mobile pattern (page 54)
- potting soil
- seeds (bean, grass, lima bean, pumpkin, or other kinds)
- various mature plants
- yarn

BOOKS TO SHARE

- *The Carrot Seed* by Ruth Krauss (Scholastic, 1974)
- *Plant Packages* by Susan Blackaby (Picture Window Books, 2003)
- *Plant Plumbing* by Susan Blackaby (Picture Window Books, 2003)
- *Planting a Rainbow* by Lois Ehlert (Harcourt Brace & Co., 1988)
- *Pumpkin Circle: The Story of a Garden* by George Levenson (Tricycle Press, 1999)

Background Information

Every flowering plant at some time produces seeds—little packages that could sprout into new plants if the growing conditions are just right. Inside of each seed are two main parts: an *embryo*, or baby plant, and a food supply called the *cotyledon*. Most seeds, such as the bean seed, have two cotyledons and their parent plants are called dicots. This is why it is easy to split open a bean seed after it has been soaked in water. Seeds with single cotyledons are produced by monocot plants, such as corn.

When a seed begins to germinate, it first absorbs water, which causes the seed to swell and burst open its outer coat. Then a tiny root starts to develop at one end of the embryo. Fine root hairs extend into the soil, anchoring the seed and pulling in more moisture to feed the tiny developing plant. Soon the embryo, or plant seedling, has popped out of the ground and is standing up "tall" to reach some sunlight. When true leaves appear, the young plant starts to produce its own food by taking in sunlight, carbon dioxide from the air, and water and minerals from the soil.

Objectives

- Identify the parts of a flowering plant: root, stem, leaf, and flower
- Observe how seeds produce plants
- Recognize that plants need sunshine, water, and space to grow

Getting Ready

- Two weeks before this activity, gather four identical plants. Place a brown paper bag over one plant and water it regularly. Remove the second plant from the dirt and place it near a sunny window on a plastic sheet and water regularly. Place the third plant in a sunny spot but do not water it. Set the fourth plant in a sunny spot and water it regularly.
- Fill a clear plastic cup with potting soil for each child. Label the cups with the children's names.
- Gather four or five mature plants (with and without flowers) that have very different leaf shapes, stems, etc., for the children to observe. Also bring vegetable produce.
- Photocopy the mobile pattern on page 54 onto card stock for each child. Cut yarn into 18 in. (46 cm) lengths, one piece for each child.
- A week or so before this activity, soak some lima beans or green bean seeds overnight and plant some in a cup of soil. Plant new seeds each day for five days, labeling each cup with the day of the week.

EXPLORATIONS • • • • • • • • • •

Looking at Plants   *What is a plant?*

There are many kinds of green plants. Show the various plants and vegetable produce that you have brought to the classroom. Have the children compare and contrast the different plants. Ask, "How are the plants different from people and other animals?" List the children's ideas on a chart.

Roots, Stems, and Leaves   *What are the parts of a plant?*

All growing plants have roots, stems, and leaves. Some plants also produce flowers and fruit. Using the bean plants you have started, remove the plants from the first and last cups you planted. Gently shake the soil off the roots. Have the children compare the two plants. (The most recently planted seedling will have one leaf and just a small root system. The more mature plant will have several leaves and many more roots.)

Science Table: Free Exploration—Invite the children to plant several kinds of vegetable and grass seeds in plastic cups and compare the growth of the plants. Have them observe how long it takes for the seeds to sprout and how different the seedlings look. *Questions to investigate:* How does a bean plant look different from grass? How does a radish plant look different from a pumpkin plant? Have the children test their ideas.

Sunlight, Water, and Soil   *What do plants need to grow and live?*

For this investigation, have the children focus on how certain kinds of plants need sunlight, water, and soil to grow. Show the children the four large plants that you have been growing for a couple of weeks. Ask them what they think may have happened to the plants that do not look like they are growing well. Explain how three of the plants were deprived of something—sunlight, water, or soil. Compare those plants with the plant that had plenty of sunlight, adequate amounts of water, and soil.

Continue the lesson by showing the young bean plants that are growing in containers. Have the children help you sequence the plants according to size. Next, arrange the plants according to the dates when they were planted. You should not have to switch very many cups. Talk about how plants that get just the right amount of sunlight, minerals from the soil, and water grow just a little bigger every day.

Invite the children to grow their own bean plants. Give each child a cup of dirt. Have the children plant two or three bean seeds in their cups. Try to plant at least one bean seed on the side of the cup so it can be seen through the clear plastic. Have the children write their names on their plant labels and stick them on the

outsides of their cups. Let the children give their seeds a small amount of water and place them in a sunny spot. Observe the plants growing over the next two weeks.

Science Center: Free Exploration—Encourage the children to think about and investigate the plants (small plants, bushes, and trees) living in their neighborhoods and natural areas to find out what is special about those plants. Record the children's observations on chart paper. *Questions to investigate:* What do leaves from various kinds of plants have in common? How are they different? Collect various kinds of leaves from trees and bushes, and place them on the science table. Provide the children with opportunities to test their ideas about leaves.

CROSS-CURRICULAR FUN

I'm a Little Bean Seed

Sing to the tune of "I'm a Little Teapot."

I'm a little bean seed, (*Pretend to hold a small seed in between thumb and forefinger.*)
Hear me toot!
Here is my stem. (*Stand stiff and tall.*)
Here is my root. (*Stomp feet.*)
When you feed me water, (*Pretend to pour water over your head.*)
I love it so! (*Wrap arms around chest and give self a hug.*)
Just put me in the sun (*Raise arms in a circle over your head.*)
And watch me grow! (*Jump up with both arms overhead.*)

Flower Mobile

Create flower mobiles to decorate the room. Give each child a copy of the flower mobile pattern. Have the children color and cut out each figure. Tape a piece of yarn to the backs of the objects in the following order: pot (at the bottom), seed, flower, water drop, sunshine (at the top). Make a loop at the top of the string and hang the mobile to display it.

- -

Name _____   Date _____

Take-Home Activity

Growing Green Plants

Dear Families,

Watching plants grow and change is really a lot of fun. During science time the past few weeks, we planted _____ seeds to watch them sprout. The young plants are now too large for the containers. Would you please help your child by finding a sunny location and a larger space for this young plant to grow? Your child may need help remembering when to water the plant. Every few days, have your child look at the plant and measure its height.

After three weeks, have your child write or draw pictures about what was discovered as this vegetable plant grew. Please send those drawings to school with your child.

Thank you for your assistance,

Flower Mobile Pattern

MAGNET MAGIC

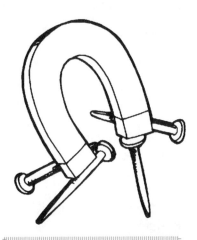

MATERIALS

- 1/2 in. (13 mm) diameter dowels cut into 6 in. (15 cm) lengths
- 1 in. (25 mm) button magnets
- 2 bar magnets
- 2 zippered plastic bags
- aluminum pie tins
- assortment of small objects (magnetic and nonmagnetic objects)
- dot stickers in two different colors
- masking tape
- materials to test: pie tin, paper plate, cardboard, tinfoil, felt, wood block, fabric, etc.
- paper clips
- pattern (page 58)
- various magnets

BOOKS TO SHARE

- *What Magnets Can Do* by Alan Fowler (Children's Press, 1995)
- *What Makes a Magnet?* by Franklyn M. Branley (HarperCollins, 1996)

Background Information

Magnets are certain objects that exhibit magnetic properties. They can be shaped like a horseshoe, button, cylinder, doughnut, or rectangular bar. Every magnet is surrounded by a magnetic field having the greatest amount of strength near the poles. When a magnet is held close to objects made of certain materials, such as nickel, iron, and steel, the objects appear to "jump" towards the magnet and cling to it. Those materials that are not attracted to magnets, known as *nonmagnetic*, include plastic, glass, paper, aluminum, gold, copper, silver, and lead. In each magnet, there are two kinds of poles, or points of concentrated strength. The like poles of magnets will repel each other, while unlike poles attract. It is important to remember that the size of a magnet is not a good indicator of its strength. The strengths of different magnets can be tested easily by holding each one near a pile of identical objects to find out how many are attracted at once.

Objectives

- Test objects to find out which ones are attracted to magnets
- Observe how like poles of magnets repel each other
- Observe how unlike poles of magnets attract each other

Getting Ready

- Write "Yes" on one zippered plastic bag and "No" on a second bag.
- Glue a round magnet to the tip of a dowel using heavy-duty epoxy glue to make a magnet "wand." Provide one wand for each group of two children in your classroom.
- Make a copy of the magnet maze on page 58 on card stock for each group of two children. To make the magnet maze: Color the maze as desired and cut it out along the solid border. Tape the maze to the bottom of a pie tin. Color the small car, bug, and people game pieces and cut out along the solid borders. Fold along the dashed lines on the people and car pieces so they will stand upright. Tape a paper clip to the bottom of each game piece.
- Prepare two identical bar magnets for the activity "Is It a Magnet?" Test the magnets by holding one end of the first magnet close to one end of the other magnet. If the ends attract, place a red sticker (for example) on the end of the first magnet and a blue sticker (for example) on the end of the second magnet. Finish the task by placing a blue sticker on the opposite end of the first magnet and a red sticker on the opposite end of the second magnet. Test the magnets again. If the ends of the magnets with matching colors repel each other, the same magnetic poles have been identified.

EXPLORATIONS • • • • • • • • •

Will It Stick? — *What will a magnet attract?*

Science Table: Free Exploration—Provide a variety of magnetic and nonmagnetic objects for the children to investigate with a magnet. Allow enough time for the children to test the various objects by holding magnets near them. As the children manipulate the magnets, talk about what they are observing.

Group Demonstration—Gather a few objects that the children have not tested with magnets. Have the children sit in a circle and discuss with them what they learned during their investigations. (A magnet is made up of a special material that is attracted to certain metal objects.) Hold up each of the objects you have gathered and have the children predict whether or not a magnet will stick to it. Then test their ideas. If the item sticks to the magnet, place it in the bag labeled "Yes." If the object is not attracted to the magnet, place it in the bag labeled "No." The children may be surprised to find out that not all objects that look like metal will be attracted to a magnet.

Science Table: Free Exploration—Send the children off as magnet detectives to find different objects that will be attracted to their magnet "wands." Alternatively, increase the strength of the magnetic force by placing two button magnets together on the wand. Have the children use their "super strong" magnets to observe what happens when the wands are close to other objects. *Note: Cover the magnets with masking tape to remind the children not to separate the button magnets.* See how many paper clips the children can pick up at one time with the magnet wands. Of course, repeat the test several times to find out if the outcome is always the same.

Magnet Mazes — *Will a magnet attract metal through another object?*

Gather an assortment of materials, such as a pie tin, a paper plate, cardboard, tinfoil, felt, a wood block, and fabric. Have the children predict whether the magnet is powerful enough to attract a paper clip through the paper, cardboard, felt, or other item. Demonstrate each material and talk about why the magnet does or does not attract the paper clip through certain substances.

Give each pair of children a maze, game piece (bug, car, or person), and magnet wand. Place the game piece on the maze where it says "Start." Encourage one child to hold the maze while the other child holds the magnet wand beneath the pie tin directly under the game piece. Ask the child to drag the game piece through the maze by maneuvering it with the magnet wand you have prepared. Alternatively, the children may make their own mazes by drawing a line to follow on a piece of paper.

Is It a Magnet? — *How can you tell if an object is a magnet?*

After exploring how a magnet is attracted only to certain materials, challenge the children to test their ideas about magnetic forces by finding out what happens when two magnets are held close together without touching. Either as a class demonstration or small group exploration, have the children test an unknown object (actually a magnet) with a known magnet. Ask, "If you turn the object so a different part of it is close to your magnet, what happens? Can you find a spot on your object where the magnet will not attract it?" Encourage the children to continue the test by turning the object in different ways and then holding the magnet close to it to observe any interaction. (One test for determining if an object is a magnet is finding out that some part of the object will repel the known magnet, while other parts are attracted to it.)

Science Table: Free Exploration—Provide bar magnets that have been labeled with colored dot stickers. Direct the children to find out what happens when the ends of the magnets with different colored stickers are placed close together. Does the same thing happen when the ends with the same colored stickers are close together? (Outcome: Like poles repel and unlike poles attract.)

CROSS-CURRICULAR FUN • • • • • • •

Sticker Attraction

To reinforce how magnets are attracted to each other, have the children play the following game. Choose two different colors of dot stickers (e.g., red and blue). Place stickers (two or three of each color) on the children's bodies, such as on the backs of hands, foreheads, knees, or elbows. Have the children dash about the play area. At your signal, the children should stop and freeze. Tell them that the stickers on their bodies are "magnets" with either a red magnetic pole or a blue magnetic pole showing. However, these sticker magnets are only attracted to sticker magnets that are the other color, just like the Law of Magnetic Poles: Like poles repel and opposite poles attract. (Red sticker magnets are attracted to blue sticker magnets and vice versa.) Have the children find partners and match "magnets" with different colors by touching the stickers together. Once everyone has found a partner, turn the sticker magnets off and resume dashing around the play area. Continue the magnet game using different criteria, such as sticking three people together at once, or see if you can stick the entire class together in one massive magnetic mess.

- -

• •

Name _____   Date _____

Take-Home Activity

Magnet Magic

Dear Families,

During science time today, we were busy exploring with magnets. It is a lot of fun looking for things that are attracted to a magnet. Would you please help your child find out if there are magnets in your house? You can check the refrigerator door with a large paper clip to find out if a magnet is used to hold the door closed. *Note: Keep all magnets away from computers to prevent damage.* What happens when two magnets are held close together?

When finished, have your child write or draw a picture about what was discovered on the back of this paper before returning it to school.

Thank you for your assistance,

Magnet Maze Pattern

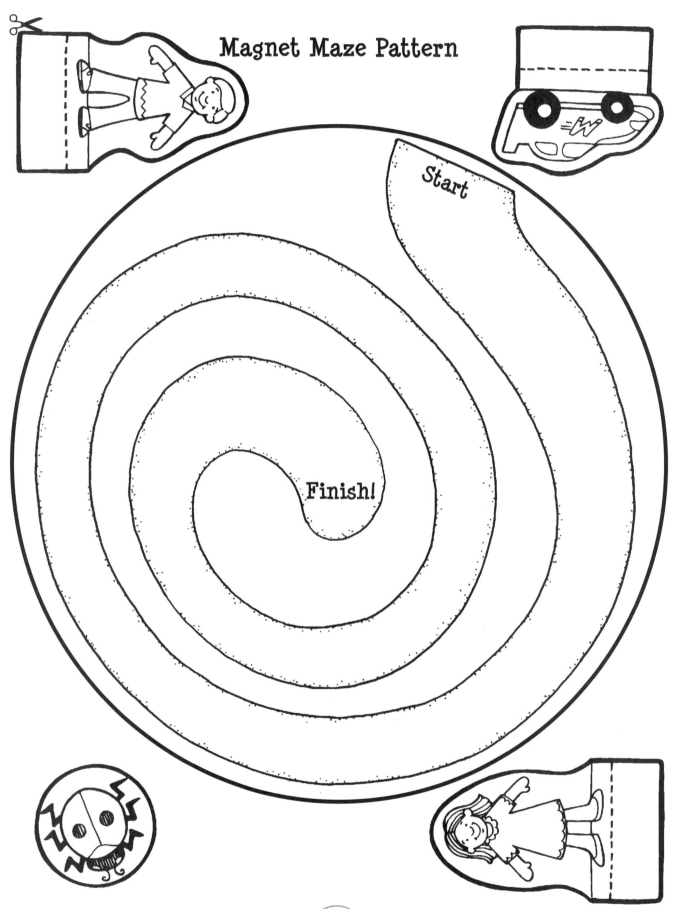

Start

Finish!

SINK OR FLOAT?

Background Information

When objects are being tested to find out if they float or sink in water, different forces are at work. As the weight of the object exerts a downward force (gravity pulling on the object), another force is pushing up against the object. This buoyant force is caused by the weight of the water that is being displaced by the object. That upward force can be felt, for example, when you push against a plastic egg that is floating on the water. When this force is greater than the object's weight, the object will float. However, if the object is denser than the water displaced, it will sink. How buoyant or "floatable" an object is actually depends on the size and shape of the object as well as its mass and density.

Objectives

• Observe how the force of water pushes up lightweight objects
• Make a prediction about what will happen when an object is placed in the water
• Classify objects by sinking or floating properties
• Change the weight of an object to make it sink
• Change the shape of an object to make it float
• Test the capacity of a clay boat

Getting Ready

• Fill the water table or a large container with water.
• Place the assortment of items (cotton balls, rice, beans, etc.) in separate containers. This makes it easier for the children to fill the plastic eggs with identical items.

EXPLORATIONS

Watch It Float!   *What floats? What sinks?*

Give each child an empty plastic egg. Let the children take turns pushing their eggs down into the water. Ask, "When you push down, what do you feel?" Talk about how the children can feel a force pushing against the plastic eggs. Now test the table tennis ball. Ask, "Will the ball float if it is placed in the water?" (Yes.) "What will happen when the golf ball is placed in the water?" (It sinks.) Have the children test their ideas. (The table tennis ball is buoyant because it is lightweight and does not displace very much water. The golf ball is not buoyant. Even though it is the same size as the table tennis ball, the golf ball is denser than water and sinks.) Repeat the test to find out if the outcome is always the same.

MATERIALS

• balance and identical units (washers, plastic counters, etc.)
• clear plastic cups
• cotton balls, dried beans, rice, pennies, and gravel
• crayons
• golf balls and table tennis balls
• modeling clay
• noisemakers
• paper
• pie tin
• plastic eggs (that can be filled)
• plastic storage containers
• salt
• spoons
• water
• water table

BOOKS TO SHARE

• *Float and Sink* by Maria Gordon (Thomson Learning, 1995)
• *Who Sank the Boat?* by Pamela Allen (Putnam, 1996)

EXPLORATIONS (CONTINUED)

Science Table: Free Exploration—Gather an assortment of objects that the children can test and classify: those that float or those that sink. Each time before an item is placed in the water, have the children make a prediction. *Note: Allow young children ample time to test the objects more than once. It is important to observe that the same outcome happens each time a certain object is placed in the water.* If appropriate, have the children draw pictures of the items that float and those that sink on chart paper.

Egg Poppers

How can a floating object be made to sink?

Science Table: Free Exploration—Show the children how to push the plastic eggs down into the water and release them so they pop back up to the surface. Ask, "How can the plastic egg be changed so that it will sink to the bottom of the container? If the egg is filled with beans, will it sink? What if it is filled with cotton balls? Rice?" Have the children test their ideas. Explore by filling the eggs with an assortment of materials to find out which things (and how many of them) are needed to sink the eggs. Show the children how to spoon the material into one half of the plastic egg and then place the other half on top to seal the egg. Before setting the egg in the water, the child should feel the egg, compare its weight with an empty egg, and make a prediction. Have the children test and retest filler items. For example, the weight of a few beans will not sink the egg, but maybe the weight of many beans will.

Crayon Sinkers and Floaters

How can you make a floater sink?

Not all crayons will sink in water! It is always fun for children to discover this outcome. To set up this experience for the children, provide a variety of crayons and a tub of water. Have the children each select a crayon and then test it to see if it is a "floater." Why do some crayons float and others sink? During the crayon manufacturing process, pigment (color) is stirred into the wax. Little pockets of air also get stirred into the wax, making some crayons more buoyant than others. If you tie two or more crayons together, you can increase their size and weight, and turn floaters into sinkers. *Questions to investigate:* Do smaller crayons float better than bigger ones? Do crayons without their wrappers float while those with wrappers sink? Are some colors more prone to floating? Provide the children with opportunities to test their ideas.

Clay Boats

If the shape of the clay is changed, will it float on water?

Discuss how large ships can float in the water because their size distributes the weight of the ship over a large area. If you were to fold the boat in half, it would sink. To demonstrate, show the children a ball of clay. Ask the them to predict what will happen if you drop the ball into the water. Then test their ideas. Note how the ball sank to the bottom of the water table. Manipulate the ball of clay so that it forms a small boat with a wide bottom. Ask the children again to predict what they think will happen to the clay. Place the boat in the water table. (The boat should float. The weight of the clay is distributed over a bigger area.)

Science Table: Free Exploration—Have the children try to create clay boats that will float. If there is a water table in the classroom, allow them to use it to test their boats. Continue the experiment with different sizes of clay boats. Also provide small, identical, plastic objects that can be transported in the boats. *Question to investigate:* How much can the clay boats hold and still float? Let the children test their ideas.

CROSS-CURRICULAR FUN • • • • • •

Moving to Sounds

Here is an action game for those times when everyone needs to move. Gather two distinct noisemakers, such as a duck call and a whistle. Place a large blanket or several sheets of craft paper on the floor to represent a pond. Tell the children that every time they hear the duck call they should "sink down" into the pond by sitting or curling their bodies into "balls" (if space permits). Whenever they hear the whistle, they should float back up to a standing position. Alternate the sounds of the two noisemakers to have the children practice the different positions. Extend the activity by having the children float or sink in degrees when they hear the appropriate noise. For example, if they hear the duck call the first time, they would just hunch their shoulders. The next time they would bend over at the waist, then crouch, sit, and finally curl into a ball. Keep on playing the game by "sinking" and "floating" until the children have worked out all their wiggles.

- -

Name _____   Date _____

Take-Home Activity

Will It Sink or Float?

Dear Families,

During science time today, we discovered how some things will float on water while others sink to the bottom of the container. Please help your child do more exploring by testing things in a sink full of water. Choose four things to test and then have your child try each one in the water two times. Does the same thing happen each time?

When finished, have your child write or draw a picture about what was discovered on the back of this paper before returning it to school.

Thank you for your asistance,

ROLLING BALLS AND SLIDING BLOCKS

MATERIALS

- 2 wood planks
- balloons
- balls (various kinds)
- bar of hard soap
- black marker
- blocks or books
- card stock
- colored chalk
- ice cubes
- magnifying glass
- masking tape
- paper
- pieces of carpet, sandpaper, or tinfoil
- poster board
- variety of shoes
- various objects to roll
- water table

BOOKS TO SHARE

- *Forces Make Things Move* by Kimberly Brubaker Bradley (HarperCollins, 2005)
- *What Is Friction?* by Lisa Trumbauer (Children's Press, 2004)

Background Information

An object will not move unless a force acts upon it. Therefore, energy is needed to make things move. Friction is the force that stops moving objects or prevents them from moving. When a ball is pushed, it will roll for a distance and then stop moving. Why does it stop? The force of friction or "stickiness" between the ball and the floor slows it down until it stops rolling. *Remember:* The smoother a surface is, the weaker the force of friction will be.

Objectives

- Observe how balls must be pushed to make them roll
- Test and classify objects by rolling or sliding properties
- Make predictions and test how balls roll across different surfaces
- Observe how friction slows down moving objects

Getting Ready

- Blow up several balloons, one for each child in class.
- Freeze enough ice cubes for everyone in class.
- Prepare a simple chart on poster board. Write the titles of the two categories: "Things That Roll" and "Things That Slide."

EXPLORATIONS

Rolling Balls   *What causes balls to roll?*

How can balls be made to move? No doubt many young children have already discovered that they must push balls to make them roll. However, they may not have compared what happens when testing different kinds of balls and rolling them on different surfaces. Locate a large, open surface for the children to use and provide different kinds of balls for them to roll at different speeds. *Questions to investigate:* Why did the balls start moving? What did you do to make the ball roll the farthest? The fastest? Do larger balls always roll farther than small balls when pushed the same way? Why did the balls stop rolling? Have the children test their ideas.

Science Table: Free Exploration—If possible, cover one-half (lengthwise) of your water table with a piece of carpeting. Elevate one end of the table to create an incline. Now allow the children to roll golf balls and table tennis balls down the length of the table to explore how the objects move differently on smooth and carpeted surfaces.

EXPLORATIONS (CONTINUED)

Will It Roll?
How will the [name of object] move down the ramp?

When young children start to build ramps in the block center, it may also be a wonderful opportunity to have them investigate how various objects move down the ramps. Provide a collection of objects for the children to test. Using blocks or books, prop a very smooth board at an incline so that certain objects will either roll or slide down its surface. Be sure to place the ramp on a carpet to slow down the movement of the objects that roll off the ramp. Have the children work in small groups. As each object is tested, place it in the appropriate category: things that roll or things that slide. Afterwards, discuss with the children why some things will roll down the ramp. Ask, "How are the things that roll the same?" (Objects such as vegetable cans, oatmeal containers, coffee cans, pencils, watercolor markers, potato chip cans, and plastic drinking glasses are all cylinders and will roll if placed on their curved sides. If the incline of the ramp is steep enough, some cylinders may also slide down when placed upright on the flat surface.)

Sliding Blocks
Why do the sliding blocks stop moving?

Sliding blocks across smooth surfaces is another interesting investigation for young children. To find out more about the outcomes, give each child an identical block to test. Ask, "How far will it slide? What can you do to make it slide even farther?" (The block will slide across the surface until friction slows it down to a stop. If the surface is rubbed with a bar of hard soap, the block will slide even farther and faster.) Have the children also test their blocks by sliding them across carpet. Ask, "What did you notice when the block slid across the carpet? Did you have to push harder against the block to make it move?" Have the children test their ideas.

Erect two identical ramps with a low incline using blocks or books and very smooth planks of wood. Stack three or four books under one end of each ramp. Have the children predict how far their blocks will slide and then test their ideas by pushing the blocks down the ramp. To mark the distance each block traveled, use a small piece of masking tape. *Question to investigate:* Will all blocks slide the same distance? To find out, give the children additional blocks of different sizes and weights to test on the ramps. To compare the outcomes, always test the original blocks on the first ramp and the new blocks on the second ramp. Remind the children to try to push the blocks the same way each time.

Science Table: Free Exploration—Provide other objects for the children to test by sliding them down the ramps. Continue the experiment with a ramp that is covered with carpet, sandpaper, or tinfoil.

Friction Walk
On what kind of surface will [name of object] slide easily?

Friction actually helps us walk across smooth and rough surfaces. Take the children on a friction walk. Investigate several different surfaces throughout the school and playground area. Stop on a carpeted surface, linoleum or tiled surface, gravel or sandy surface, grass, pavement, etc. Have the children slide their feet back and forth each time. Which surface feels the smoothest? (The smoother the surface, the less friction there will be.) Ask the children, "Why is it important to know how slippery a floor is?"

Science Table: Free Exploration—Using a magnifying lens, have the children compare the soles of different shoes: tennis shoes, dress shoes, ballet slippers, work boots, hiking boots, rain boots, and so on.

CROSS-CURRICULAR FUN

Friction Rhythm

Have the children sit on chairs over a tiled or linoleum surface with their feet touching the floor. Invite them to listen and mimic your "friction rhythm." To create a rhythm, slide one or both of your feet back and forth on the smooth surface. Now encourage the children to repeat the rhythm with their own feet. Alternatively, rub hands on legs for added rhythm fun.

Ice Cube Art

Ice cubes melt while sitting in a warm location. They melt even faster when friction is applied. Place one ice cube on the sidewalk. Give each child an ice cube, too. Have the children predict what will happen when they rub their ice cubes on the sidewalk. Then conduct the investigation. As the children rub their ice cubes on the cement, ask them to compare their ice cubes (that are being reduced by friction) with the ice cube that is simply melting. Which one is melting faster?

Extend the ice-melting lesson into an art project. Have the children each draw a picture on construction paper with chalk. The more chalk that is used, the better this process will work. Once the pictures are colored, direct the children to take ice cubes and rub them over their pictures. The melting ice will create a water-colored effect with the chalk drawings.

Name _____   Date _____

Take-Home Activity

Rolling Balls and Soda Bottle Game

Dear Families,

During science time today, we discovered that energy is needed to make things move. That means we must push or pull things to start them moving. As large and small balls roll across a floor, the force of friction slows them down until they stop moving. Please help your child do more exploring about how things move by rolling a ball to knock down two large, plastic soda bottles. First, have your child work with empty bottles. Then try again with bottles that are filled halfway with water and sealed tightly with caps.

When finished, have your child write or draw a picture about what was discovered on the back of this paper before returning it to school.

Thank you for your assistance,